LEGENDS

THE BEST PLAYERS, GAMES, AND TEAMS IN

FOOTBALL

HOWARD BRYANT

PUFFIN BOOKS

PUFFIN BOOKS
An imprint of Penguin Random House LLC
375 Hudson Street
New York, New York 10014

First published in the United States of America by Philomel Books,
an imprint of Penguin Random House LLC, 2015
Published by Puffin Books, an imprint of Penguin Random House LLC, 2016

LIBRARY OF CONGRESS CATALOGING-IN-PUBLICATION DATA IS AVAILABLE.

ISBN 9780399169045 (HC)
Puffin Books ISBN 9780147512567

Printed in the United States of America

7 9 10 8 6

Edited by Michael Green.   Design by Semadar Megged.

PHOTO CREDITS

Cover: Football, Copyright © David Lee/Shutterstock   Chapter openers: Goalpost
copyright © Kostsov/Shutterstock, Football copyright © VitaminCo/Shutterstock
Insert: Green Bay Packers: Copyright © Neil Leifer/Neil Leifer Collection/Getty Images
Joe Namath: Copyright © Walter Iooss Jr./Sports Illustrated Classic/Getty Images
Larry Csonka: Copyright © Walter Iooss Jr./Sports Illustrated/Getty Images   Sports
Illustrated cover: Copyright © Heinz Kluetmeier/Sports Illustrated/Getty Images Ken
Stabler and John Madden: Copyright © Neil Leifer/Neil Leifer Collection/Getty Images
"Mean" Joe Greene and Jack Ham: Copyright © Focus On Sport/Getty Images Sport/
Getty Images Bill Walsh: Copyright © Walter Iooss Jr./Sports Illustrated/Getty Images
Buddy Ryan: Copyright © Kidwiler Collection/Diamond Images/Getty Images Doug
Williams: Copyright © AP Images Jerry Rice: Copyright © Heinz Kluetmeier/Sports
Illustrated/Getty Images Joe Montana: Copyright © David Madison/Getty Images
Sport Classic/Getty Images Michael Irvin, Troy Aikman, and Emmitt Smith: Copyright
© Jeff Haynes/AFP/Getty Images Brett Favre and John Elway: Copyright © AP Images
Kevin Dyson: Copyright © AP Images Tom Brady hit by Charles Woodson: Copyright
© Boston Globe/Getty Images Tom Brady, Super Bowl XXXVIII: Copyright © Walter
Iooss Jr./Sports Illustrated/Getty Images David Tyree: Copyright © Andy Lyons/Getty
Images Sport Classic/Getty Images Eli Manning: Copyright © Gabriel Bouys/AFP/Getty
Images Ben Roethlisberger: Copyright © Lexington Herald-Leader/Tribune News
Service/ Getty Images Drew Brees: Copyright © Rob Tringali/SportsChrome/ Getty
Images Mario Manningham: Copyright © Win McNamee/ Getty Images Sport/Getty
Images Malcolm Butler intercepts Russell Wilson: Copyright © John Iacono/Sports
Illustrated/Getty Images

For Simone Hughes, a great friend to the young people just starting their journey

Contents

A Note from Howard Bryant   *ix*

First Down: 1! 3! 7! 10! 11! Hutt! Hutt!

Super Bowl I, A New Day:

     Green Bay Packers vs. Kansas City Chiefs   *3*

Super Bowl III, The Upset:

     New York Jets vs. Baltimore Colts   *13*

Super Bowl VII, The Undefeated:

     Miami Dolphins vs. Washington   *25*

Super Bowl X, The Best Yet:

     Pittsburgh Steelers vs. Dallas Cowboys   *37*

Super Bowl XI, The Bad Guys Win:

     Oakland Raiders vs. Minnesota Vikings   *49*

Second Down: 13! 16! 20! 22! 24! Hutt! Hutt!

Super Bowl XIII, The Rematch, Part I:

     Pittsburgh Steelers vs. Dallas Cowboys   *63*

Super Bowl XVI, The Dawn of a Dynasty:

     San Francisco 49ers vs. Cincinnati Bengals   *75*

Super Bowl XX, The Demolition:

     Chicago Bears vs. New England Patriots   *89*

Super Bowl XXII, The Pioneer:

     Washington vs. Denver Broncos   *105*

Super Bowl XXIV, Perfection:

San Francisco 49ers vs. Denver Broncos   *119*

THIRD DOWN: 27! 32! 34! 36! 38! HUTT! HUTT!

Super Bowl XXVII, The Return of the Star:

Dallas Cowboys vs. Buffalo Bills   *135*

Super Bowl XXXII, Finally, a Champion:

Denver Broncos vs. Green Bay Packers   *151*

Super Bowl XXXIV, The Greatest Show on Turf:

St. Louis Rams vs. Tennessee Titans   *166*

Super Bowl XXXVI, An Unlikely Dynasty is Born:

New England Patriots vs. St. Louis Rams   *181*

Super Bowl XXXVIII, And Then There Were Two . . . :

New England Patriots vs. Carolina Panthers   *200*

FOURTH DOWN: 42! 43! 44! 46! 49! HUTT! HUTT!

Super Bowl XLII, A Giant Upset:

New York Giants vs. New England Patriots   *217*

Super Bowl XLIII, Winning and Losing—By a Hair:

Pittsburgh Steelers vs. Arizona Cardinals   *232*

Super Bowl XLIV, Score One for the Underdogs:

New Orleans Saints vs. Indianapolis Colts   *244*

Super Bowl XLVI, The Rematch, Part II:

New York Giants vs. New England Patriots   *257*

Super Bowl XLIX, One to Remember, One to Forget:

    Seattle Seahawks vs. New England Patriots   *270*

A TIMELINE OF FOOTBALL'S KEY MOMENTS (TOP 40 STYLE)   *288*

PHOTOS

INDEX   *293*

A Note from Howard Bryant

This might come as a total shock, but when I was a kid, my favorite thing about playing football was . . . fear.

In a lot of ways, I loved being afraid. My friends and I used to play football, or when we had too many kids for that, a game called "pig pile," where one person carried the football and all the other players chased and tried to tackle him. When he was finally brought to the ground, he would toss the ball up in the air and some other brave soul would pick it up and run for as long as possible before *he* was tackled.

When I was the one being chased, every second was filled with the fear of being taken down hard to the ground.

But here's the part that made being afraid fun. Are you ready? It was laughing at the fear!

I know that might seem odd, so let me explain: We all know the goal of football is to score touchdowns and prevent the other team from scoring. Defenses love trying to intimidate offenses. I played running back, wide receiver, and even quarterback sometimes. I remember how big some of the other kids were. I remember how they would stand on the other side of the line and try to scare me.

You are a dead man if you touch that ball. I'm gonna squash you like a bug . . .

The quarterback would hand me the ball and I would see the defense race toward me, charging and snarling. Here they came, trying to make good on their promises to indeed squash me like a bug, and the fear would kick in.

So I ran.

And I dodged.

And I spun.

And I realized that I was *fast*! I would score a touchdown and the guys who told me I was a dead man would get mad because not only was I very much alive, but my team was winning and theirs was losing!

So yeah, big kids were stronger than me, but I was faster. Even so, sometimes I got hit, and they would smile and talk trash while I was down (*Who's smiling now?*), but I always got up. What started as an exercise in fear turned into a little game of me betting that I could be faster than everyone. And, when necessary, proving I could take a hit and still get back up.

These were the challenges of football. Speed against strength. Fear against courage. I loved it all. And it was just as much fun to watch on TV as it was to play, for so many reasons.

I loved the NFL uniforms, particularly the helmets. I grew up in Boston and the original Patriots logo was the hardest logo in sports to draw. Believe me—I tried a lot.

Most of all, I loved the competition, the way the Steelers, Dolphins, Raiders, Vikings, and Cowboys ruled the game and always seemed to end up having to beat each other to get to the Super Bowl. My childhood team, the Patriots, could never beat those other guys, but I rooted for them just the same.

I rooted for players because I loved how they moved, how the really fast guys would just break away from defenders after a long reception, reach the end zone, and dance in celebration. The Dallas Cowboys became my adoptive team because I loved the great quarterback Roger Staubach and running back Tony Dorsett. Later, I couldn't help but admire the historic

San Francisco 49ers dynasty of the 1980s, the way their innovative offense and always-cool quarterback Joe Montana seemed unstoppable whenever a game was on the line.

The game has continued to change over the years. When I was a kid, I used to come home from playing football with my shirt ripped and my clothing covered in dirt and grass stains. My friends and I played tackle with no helmets, and even if you banged heads with another kid, people just told us to "shake it off." Today we know that the players are so strong that getting hit and tackled that many times hurts not just the body but the brain. There is no such thing as a minor injury to the brain. Because we understand more about these injury risks, because the game is potentially so dangerous, many parents no longer let their kids play football the way I used to. So while I still enjoy watching the game on TV, more than anything these days I hope that the skilled people playing it remain safe.

Other shifts in attitude have taken place, as well. Some of the sport's traditions are no longer acceptable in today's society. For example, even though "Redskins" is still the nickname of the Washington football team, I do not use that word in this book because I consider it to be offensive to all people of Native American descent, as well as demeaning to the people using the term. Throughout the book, therefore, I refer to the team as "Washington."

This is a book not only of football legends—but of the legend of pro football. It is this country's most popular sport. While the game has been played since the late 1800s, for the sake of this book we begin when two rival leagues, the National Football League and the American Football League, became one in 1970. The only exception to this rule can be found in the Timeline of Football's Key Moments at the end of the book, which includes older events that were too important to leave out. Above all else, though, this book is a tribute to the Super Bowl, which began as a little-watched championship between the two leagues in 1967, only to evolve into the most popular sporting event in America. And it continues to evolve—2016 marks the first Super Bowl that will be numbered with Arabic numerals (i.e. "Super Bowl 50") instead of Roman numerals ("Super Bowl L"), which have been in use since the first Super Bowl.

Through the lens of the Super Bowl, this book is

about the rise of dynasties and the fall of giants. If the book had been written thirty years ago, for instance, the Miami Dolphins would've been a really big part of it and the Patriots wouldn't have been mentioned at all, because back then Miami was so good . . . and the Patriots? The Patriots were gum on the bottom of your shoe, stepped on by everyone.

Times change, and now the Patriots are one of the great franchises in history. Miami, meanwhile, hasn't been to a Super Bowl since 1984 and hasn't won one since 1973.

In the NFL, it's all about the Super Bowl.

FIRST DOWN

SUPER BOWL I
A NEW DAY

GREEN BAY PACKERS VS.
KANSAS CITY CHIEFS

There was nothing super about Super Bowl I. The biggest game of the year wasn't even called the Super Bowl at first. That would come later. Before there was the National Football League as we know it today, two leagues coexisted, sometimes in the same city, and they didn't like each other. The first was the National Football League, founded in 1920 and—save for a brief rival league called the AAFC in the 1940s that created the Baltimore Colts, San Francisco 49ers, and Cleveland Browns—they went unchallenged as the only professional football league in America for forty years.

The second was the American Football League, founded in 1960 as a challenger to the NFL. It brought the sport to cities like Boston, Kansas City, Denver, and Houston that did not have pro football teams in the National Football League.

Football off the field in the 1960s was dominated by the AFL-NFL rivalry. The NFL laughed at the new league, because surely it was inferior to the great teams of the NFL. But over the next few years, the AFL gained credibility and popularity, and soon enough, the heads of the two leagues began to discuss the idea of a merger.

They came to an agreement in 1966, keeping their regular season schedules separate for four years, but bound together by a championship game—a face-off between the AFL champion and NFL champion. The championship game would be called the "AFL-NFL World Championship Game," and the inaugural game was played in Los Angeles, on January 15, 1967, at the Los Angeles Memorial Coliseum.

The Green Bay Packers were the dominant team in the NFL during the 1960s. There were other strong teams, such as the Cleveland Browns, led by the great running back Jim Brown, and the Baltimore Colts, led by legendary quarterback Johnny Unitas, but the Packers always seemed to end the season on top.

The leader of the pack was the legendary coach Vince Lombardi, who relied on his outstanding play-caller, hall-of-fame quarterback Bart Starr. Max McGee, a terrific receiver, was Starr's go-to wideout. In the backfield, Green Bay had not one, but two great running backs: the physical fullback Jim Taylor and the versatile halfback Paul Hornung.

Defensively, the Packers were just as stacked, with a dangerous defensive line led by Forrest Gregg, a fearsome middle linebacker in Ray Nitschke, and an unforgiving secondary that featured cornerback Herb Adderley and safety Willie Wood.

The Packers had won the NFL championship in 1961, 1962, and 1965, and they entered the first year of the Super Bowl as heavy favorites to represent the National Football League.

Today, as you know, NFL teams throw the football a lot. Peyton Manning drops back to pass and has three, four, and sometimes five receivers to look for. Tom Brady will drop back into the "shotgun" formation, 5 yards behind the center, to get a better look at the defense and buy some time before they reach him.

In the 1960s, Lombardi's Packers were a power running team that mixed in some passing elements. The 1966 team was nearly last in the league in passing attempts, which upset Starr, who wanted to throw the ball—as all quarterbacks do. They were famous for the "Packer Sweep," during which Starr would snap the ball and the offensive line would block to the left while Taylor or Hornung or their newest back, Elijah Pitts, ran behind. The skilled line would create a human wall for the running backs, engulfing the defense in a show of sheer power. By the fourth quarter, with defenses beat up and tired from an afternoon of being pounded by the Packers line, Lombardi, a relentless foe, would continue to run the ball, leaving defenses gasping for air and eventually surrendering large chunks of yardage. It was a strategy that worked time and time again.

NFL seasons were fourteen games long in these days, not sixteen, like we have today. The Packers went 12-2 in 1966, including one dominant stretch in which they crushed the Bears (17–0), the Falcons (56–3) and the Lions (31–7)—a combined score of 104–10!

The year of the first Championship Game, the

Packers played Dallas in the NFL title game. The Cowboys were founded in 1960 and in a very short time, under the guidance of another legendary coach, Tom Landry, made a fast rise to prominence. Landry was a defensive coach. He and Lombardi had coached together in the 1950s with the New York Giants. Landry had been the defensive coordinator, and Lombardi the offensive coach, but Landry's Cowboys were a high-scoring, high-offense team, scoring 30 points or more in half of their games—and twice reaching 50! They had a flamboyant quarterback in "Dandy" Don Meredith, and perhaps the fastest man in football, wide receiver "Bullet" Bob Hayes, who was so fast, he was once a sprinter in the Olympics.

So it was the ground-and-pound attack of Lombardi and the defending champion Packers against the high-flying attack of Landry's upstart Cowboys. The genius of Lombardi, though, wasn't just his passion to win, but his ability to find weaknesses in an opponent and beat them at their own game. So when the Packers played the Cowboys in the title game, they didn't rely on running the football, like they usually did. Instead, they changed up their strategy, passing the ball the way Dallas had all season. Starr, so often frustrated that Lombardi never seemed to let him throw the ball, threw 4 touchdowns.

The Packers ended up beating the Cowboys 34–27. At 13-2, they were headed to the first-ever Super Bowl. Their opponents? The AFL's Kansas City Chiefs.

Coincidentally, the Chiefs began life in Dallas as the Dallas Texans. They had won the AFL title in 1962 and then moved to Kansas City. Their quarterback, Len Dawson, had been a career backup in the NFL when he jumped leagues and joined the Texans in 1962, giving him a second chance to be a pro starter. In the AFL, Dawson showed he was an accurate passer and team leader. He was arguably the best quarterback in the AFL, which was proof to some that he only needed to be given a chance to succeed. To others, though, Dawson being the best quarterback only showed that the AFL was a weak league. Naturally, in Super Bowl I, Dawson had something to prove.

The Chiefs running back, Mike Garrett, a Heisman Trophy–winning star during his time at the University of Southern California, had said no to an invitation to join the NFL, boldly choosing to play in the AFL instead. Together with Dawson and talented wide receiver Otis Taylor, the Chiefs were an offensive machine. They averaged more than 30 points per game, and their 448 total points were 90 points more than Buffalo's, the next closest team. The Chiefs could score on the ground or in the air, but it was the arm of Dawson that powered them.

They went through the regular season untroubled, and faced Buffalo in the AFL title game. The Bills sacked Dawson 9 times, yet the Chiefs still crushed them 31–7, making them the first AFL representatives in the inaugural Super Bowl.

The announced crowd at the Los Angeles Memorial Coliseum was 61,946, which wasn't even a sellout. Today, Katy Perry or Beyoncé headline the halftime show. For this game, the University of Michigan and University of Arizona marching bands provided the entertainment.

Today, a thirty-second television commercial costs nearly $2.5 million. In 1967, the cost was $42,000. The game was televised on both NBC and CBS. Today, cable and broadcast channels pay billions of dollars to take turns televising the event.

After a tightly-fought first quarter at 7–7, the Packers took a 14–10 lead before halftime and never looked back. The Chiefs wouldn't score again for the rest of the game. As much as the AFL desperately wanted to win, to show the NFL that they belonged on the same field as the NFL's best, the Packers overwhelmed them, 35–10.

Green Bay would continue to be the dominant team next season, again representing the NFL in the second AFL-NFL World Championship Game. Super Bowl II was barely more competitive than the first one, as the Packers destroyed the Oakland Raiders 33–14 and solidified themselves as the team of the 1960s with five championships, and Lombardi as one of the great coaches of all time. The dynasty would end there, however, as the Packers would not reach another championship for nearly thirty years. Lombardi's Packers, though, never fully faded into memory. They were so great, and Lombardi's influence so powerful, that the trophy would later be renamed the Vince Lombardi Trophy. The championship trophy retains that name to this day.

The game was a dud, but it had a new nickname, the kind that stuck: The AFL-NFL World Championship was dead. The Super Bowl was born.

SUPER BOWL I
TOP TEN LIST

More than any other sport, football is where coaching makes the biggest difference. The great coaches in football are as iconic as the players. Here is a list of the greatest coaches in the Super Bowl era.

1. Vince Lombardi—Green Bay Packers: Won Super Bowls I and II. Championship trophy named after him.
2. Tom Landry—Dallas Cowboys: Won Super Bowls VI and XII. Coached the Cowboys to five Super Bowls.
3. Bill Belichick—New England Patriots: Has won four Super Bowls as a coach (thus far) and two more as an assistant.
4. Don Shula—Baltimore Colts, Miami Dolphins: All-time winningest head coach in NFL history.

Won two Super Bowls, including Super Bowl VII,
the 17-0 1972 Dolphins.

5. Joe Gibbs—Washington: Won three Super Bowls
   with three different quarterbacks.

6. Bill Parcells—New York Giants, New England
   Patriots, New York Jets, Dallas Cowboys: Won
   two Super Bowls with New York Giants. Coached
   a third with the Patriots in 1996, a loss to the
   Packers.

7. Bill Walsh—San Francisco 49ers: Great offensive
   innovator and champion. Won three Super
   Bowls. Architect of a 49ers dynasty.

8. Chuck Noll—Pittsburgh Steelers: Leader of the
   Steel Curtain dynasty. Winner of four Super
   Bowls.

9. Jimmy Johnson—Dallas Cowboys, Miami
   Dolphins: Innovative coach who won two Super
   Bowls with Dallas.

10. Marv Levy—Kansas City Chiefs, Buffalo Bills:
    Did not win a championship, but he was the
    only coach in history to reach four straight Super
    Bowls (with the Bills).

SUPER BOWL III
THE UPSET

~~~~~~

New York Jets vs.
Baltimore Colts

There's nothing worse in the world than being around those kids who act like they're better than you. Maybe they're more popular, or just think they are. Or maybe you're the new kid, and new kids never catch a break. The new kid has to prove he belongs.

That's how the coaches and players of the American Football League felt in 1968. Even though the decision to merge with the NFL had been made three years earlier, even though both sides had agreed that, beginning in 1970, the two leagues would become one, the old established NFL still treated the AFL as if they were second-class citizens. The NFL had the famous teams, like the Green Bay Packers, Chicago Bears, Baltimore Colts, and New York Giants. They had teams that were in the big cities like Cleveland, San Francisco, and Los Angeles. The NFL had been around since 1920, forty years longer than the AFL.

Most importantly, when the two leagues did agree to merge and play a "Super Bowl" of the AFL champion against the NFL champion, the first two Super Bowls were wipeouts. The powerhouse Green Bay Packers just crushed the AFL not once, but twice. And if the Packers could cream the AFL's best teams so easily, maybe the league really *was* inferior.

To the popular teams of the NFL, the new kids in the AFL weren't worth their time.

But then, one day, on January 12, 1969, in Miami, all of the talk went away. Actually, the conversation simply changed. In a big-time way.

Joe Namath—the quarterback of the Jets, the AFL champions headed to their first Super Bowl—made a guarantee: The New York Jets would win the game. It was a bold move for one of the new kids on the block. Some would say "absurd" is a better word than "bold."

Namath was a young star quarterback out of the University of Alabama, where he had played for the legendary coach Paul "Bear" Bryant. Namath was brash. He loved to brag about how talented he was, but he backed it up, because he really was fantastic. He not only had a super-strong arm, he would release the ball very quickly, before the defensive line could hit him and before the defensive backs could adjust to defend the routes of the receivers they were covering.

When he came out of college, everyone expected Namath to sign with the NFL and to become a star. The St. Louis Cardinals drafted Namath with the twelfth pick in the first round.

But then the New York Jets drafted him with the first overall pick in the AFL draft, and just to let the world know the new league was serious about having star talent, they offered Namath a record $427,000 contract! A HUGE salary for 1965!

Namath was the magnetic star the AFL needed, and he loved that the league was counting on him to be its main attraction. He would get to play in New York, the biggest city in America. He was such a character, such a reflection of the oversized personality that is New York City, that he earned the great nickname "Broadway Joe." He wore a fur coat and frequently appeared on TV, even becoming the host of his own program, *The Joe Namath Show*, in 1969. Here was a quarterback born for the spotlight, on the field and off.

On the field, he became THE player to watch. In his third season, he became the first player in pro football history to throw for 4,000 yards in a season. The Jets had never enjoyed a winning season before Namath arrived, but with him at the helm, they transformed into AFL contenders.

The Jets had also two big, powerful running backs, Emerson Boozer and Matt Snell, who were central in helping the team lead the league in rushing touchdowns. Two clutch receivers, Don Maynard and George Sauer, who both went over 1,100 yards receiving in multiple seasons, rounded out the high-scoring offense.

As good as the offense was, their defense might have been even better. In their Super Bowl season, New York led the AFL in fewest total yards allowed, fewest rushing yards allowed, and fewest yards allowed per attempt. Teams had real difficulty scoring on them. They finished the regular season with a record of 11-3.

There was only one round of playoffs back then, featuring the two division winners. New York would face the powerful Oakland Raiders in the AFL title game, a rematch against one of the few teams who had beaten them, 43–32, in the regular season. It was a close game, but the Jets rode a late Namath rally to beat the Raiders 27–23.

The Jets, on the confident shoulders of Namath, had carved out a path to the Super Bowl—a path that landed them against the Baltimore Colts, one of the best, most storied teams from the NFL. The Colts would one day abandon the city of Baltimore for Indianapolis, but back in 1969, Baltimore was a team that football fans everywhere knew. They knew them by that classic helmet with the blue horseshoe, and the black football shoes they wore with their white uniforms. They knew them for the championships they won in 1957 and 1958. Not only were the Colts the famed team that beat the New York Giants in the 1958 NFL title game, the classic championship that earned the nickname "The Greatest Game Ever

Played," but they were also home to some of the best players ever to grace the league, like Raymond Berry, John Mackey, and Bubba Smith. Yet none of those greats could rival the star power of Johnny Unitas. Unitas, or Johnny U, as he was known, was arguably the greatest quarterback of his time, a ten-time Pro Bowl player and three-time Most Valuable Player Award winner. Unitas was the guy who made kids like Joe Namath want to play quarterback.

The Colts had a record of 13-1 in 1968, which was even more remarkable because they had earned it *without* Unitas, who had injured his arm in the team's final preseason game. Earl Morrall, the 34-year-old veteran, stepped up and played terrific football, starting in place of the injured star. But it was the Baltimore ground attack and defense that proved to be the real difference-makers. Baltimore scored 402 total points and allowed only 144 all season. The key to the Colts' defense was their blitz, when they would rush more defenders than the offensive line could block. The blitz was a great strategy because the defense rushed so many guys, the quarterback didn't have time to think before getting pressured, hurried, and sacked. Sometimes the coach, Don Shula, another one of the great coaches in football history, would line up all eleven men on the line of scrimmage to make the offense think he was going to send every player after the quarterback.

But the blitz could be risky, because rushing the quarterback with a lot of players meant there would be offensive players open if the blitz didn't reach the quarterback in time.

With Baltimore, it usually did.

The Colts won their first five games before losing 30–20 at home to Cleveland, and then went on a mad defensive tear that earned them eight straight wins to end the season. In the first seven of those matchups, no team scored more than 10 points.

They shut out the Giants 26–0.

They shut out the Cardinals 27–0.

They shut out the Falcons 44–0.

In the NFL title game at Cleveland, against the only team that had beaten them during the regular season, they shut out the Browns 34–0. Revenge was sweet. And clearly, the NFL's best team was headed to the Super Bowl.

What chance did the Jets, a team that had never won a playoff game before 1968, playing for a league that had gotten trounced in the first two Super Bowls, have against the awesome might of the Baltimore Colts?

None, if you believed most people. Even the odds-makers made the Jets 19-point underdogs. 19 points! It was as though people thought the Colts would be facing a college team.

And yet, there was Namath. And his guarantee of victory.

Days before the game, Johnny Sample, the New York Jets defensive captain, received a call in his hotel room. It was Namath.

Namath told Sample, "I just said something that's going to be all over the news tomorrow."

"What did you say?" Sample replied.

"I guaranteed we're gonna win the game."

"Aw, man," Sample said. "You didn't say that."

"Yeah," Namath said. "Yeah, I did."

He did. And football fans everywhere ate it up.

When the game started, the Colts were convinced they were going to shut Namath's loud mouth with some big hits. But it didn't quite work out as Baltimore expected. The Colts brought the pressure and Namath got the ball out of his hand so quickly, the Jets were able to move the ball against a defense that had been nearly impenetrable all season long. Yet the Colts' defense still managed to keep the Jets off the scoreboard.

After a scoreless first quarter, Morrall was intercepted with the Colts driving. Namath didn't waste a second taking advantage of the momentum shift, moving the Jets downfield, hitting Sauer on quick routes to negate the blitz. When the Jets weren't passing, Snell ate up yards on the ground, running through the Colts' defense like they were nothing but Swiss cheese. Snell ended up scoring the first touchdown of the game.

It would also be the Jets' last touchdown of the game, but their defense made it count. After an interception of a Morrall pass, the Jets tacked on a field goal, and then added another to take a 13–0 lead at halftime.

The Jets added one more field goal in the third quarter, and the great Baltimore Colts, the team that had dominated so many teams all year, the team that had shut out four teams, were getting a taste of their own medicine, falling behind 16–0.

So Shula brought in an ailing Unitas, hoping the

great man could mount a comeback, but it was too late. The Colts scored a touchdown with 3:32 left in the game to avoid the embarrassment of being shut out in a Super Bowl (which still hasn't happened to this day), but the Jets had done it. They'd become the first AFL team to win the Super Bowl.

The final score was 16–7. Broadway Joe had made good on his promise.

The next year was the final one for the AFL and NFL before they merged, and in Super Bowl IV, the AFL proved that the Jets beating the Colts was not just a single stroke of luck when Kansas City played Minnesota and crushed them, 23–7.

The rivalry was over. The AFL and NFL played four Super Bowls and had split them. The old AFL teams would become part of the NFL, playing in the new American Football Conference, or AFC, but after Super Bowl IV the AFL logo would disappear forever. When it left, it left with dignity, no longer bullied or feeling inferior to the NFL.

SUPER BOWL III
TOP TEN LIST

Broadway Joe brought the championship home to New York, but his flamboyance opened the door for many after him to show a little bit more of their own personality and style, on and off the field. With style come nicknames. Here are some of the best . . .

1. Broadway Joe (quarterback Joe Namath)
2. White Shoes Johnson (wide receiver / punt and kick returner Billy Johnson)
3. Minister of Defense (defensive end Reggie White—a Hall of Famer *and* an ordained minister)
4. Joe Cool (quarterback Joe Montana)
5. Mean Joe Greene (defensive end Joe Greene)
6. Too Tall Jones (defensive end Ed Jones)
7. Toast (defensive back Elvis Patterson—

because receivers had a tendency to burn him deep)

8. Prime Time (defensive back Deion Sanders)
9. The Assassin (defensive back Jack Tatum)
10. Sweetness (running back Walter Payton)

SUPER BOWL VII
THE UNDEFEATED

MIAMI DOLPHINS VS. WASHINGTON

There are years when a champion is crowned and everyone knows the best team didn't win. In fact, it happens all the time. Most coaches tell their players, "You don't have to be the best team. You just have to be the best team on that day." It is a saying to remind players that when two teams step onto the field, anything is possible. On any day, anyone can win.

1972 was not one of those years. The Miami Dolphins were the best team in the NFL and they were so good, they did something no team in the NFL had done since the AFL and NFL merged and that no pro football team had done since 1948: they went undefeated.

The root of the Dolphins' dominance was the pain of the season before, when the Dallas Cowboys embarrassed them 24–3 in Super Bowl VI. They returned the following year more determined than ever to go all the way.

How good were the 1972 Miami Dolphins? They were so good that:

They were the best offensive team in the league.

They were the best defensive team in the league.

They had the biggest gap between points scored and points allowed.

They had not one, but *two* 1,000-yard rushers in Larry Csonka and Mercury Morris (at a time when teams played a fourteen-game schedule only).

Their coach, Don Shula, had recently coached the mighty Baltimore Colts, leading them to the Super Bowl. In Baltimore, Shula had the NFL's best quarterback in Johnny Unitas, but when Unitas was injured, it was the backup Earl Morrall who had led the Colts to the Super Bowl. So when Shula took over in Miami, he wisely brought Morrall with him, a decision that paid off big when the Dolphins quarterback, Bob Griese, broke his ankle in Week 5. It was Morrall to the rescue again, as the Dolphins kept on rolling.

They had won those first five games of the season, and didn't miss a step with Morrall. After a close win over the Bills in Week 6, the Dolphins shut out the Colts 23–0 and kept going. A thumping of the Patriots, 52–0, brought them to 9-0.

Miami was so dominant that they trailed entering the fourth quarter only *twice* during the season, against Minnesota and the Jets, and both times the Dolphins came back to win.

They ended the regular season with a perfect 14-0 record, accomplishing what had never been done before (and has only been done once since)—going undefeated in the regular season.

Yet championships aren't won during the regular season. The Dolphins now had to remain unbeaten through the playoffs, and the pressure mounted. Losing was no longer an option. The pain of losing the Super Bowl the previous season to Dallas was one thing, but going the whole season undefeated only to lose in the playoffs would be heartbreaking.

When the playoffs began, that possibility stared Miami right in the face. The Dolphins, playing at home, faced a tough Cleveland Browns team that had finished the season 10-4. The Browns led 14–13 with eight minutes to play. Miami kept its composure, though, just as it had done throughout the season. Earl Morrall, cool as a cucumber, led the Dolphins 80 yards, and running back Jim Kiick finished off the drive with a touchdown.

Down 20–14, the Browns had one final chance to pull off the biggest upset in football, but the Miami defense saved the day, intercepting Cleveland quarterback Mike Phipps for the fifth time that day to seal the win.

In Pittsburgh for the AFC Championship Game, the Dolphins rediscovered their regular-season magic and beat the Steelers, 27–10. They were now 16-0 on the season and advanced to their second consecutive Super Bowl.

Waiting for the Dolphins was an unlikely opponent, Washington, a team that had been known for losing. They were led by George Allen, an energetic, lifelong football coach who taught his underdog players to believe in themselves, even if no one else did. The result was a team that was as close as a football team could be.

Allen arrived in 1971 and immediately set out on reshaping his football team. Most teams rebuild through the college draft, trying to acquire young players who will grow into good players. Yet Allen didn't want to wait for rookies to develop into experienced players; he wanted to win immediately, so he traded for veteran players who already had pro experience, like quarterback Billy Kilmer, who was thirty-two years old when he arrived from New Orleans. Kilmer's backup was Sonny Jurgensen, who was thirty-eight. In 1971, Allen traded for so many players that his first-year team was the oldest in the NFL, earning them the nickname "The Over-the-Hill Gang."

But Allen had the last laugh. In 1971, the year before their Super Bowl matchup against the Dolphins, Washington had won nine games, their most since 1942, and only the second time they had a winning record since 1955. And even though they ended up being eliminated by San Francisco, it was the first time Washington had made the playoffs since 1955.

Allen set his sights even higher in 1972, and his team was 11-1 before losing the last two games of the season, a suggestion that maybe the Over-the-Hill Gang, true to their nickname, had run out of gas. Division rival Dallas avenged an earlier loss and beat Washington 34–24, and then Buffalo beat them to end the season, when a spectacular running back named O. J. Simpson rushed for 101 yards and a touchdown in a 24–17 win.

Yet Washington was far from finished. They destroyed Green Bay and then Dallas in the playoffs, giving up only 6 points total, and were on their way to the Super Bowl. The belief of Allen's players, from wide receiver Charley Taylor (who would one day make the Hall of Fame) to defensive tackle Diron Talbert, was unshakeable. Before games, Allen would gather his team and tell them, "Forty men working together can't lose!"

Miami had other thoughts. The team that had been so dominant throughout the regular season showed why. Washington did not score a single point on offense. Kilmer's magic had run out, as he was intercepted three times by the Dolphins' defense.

But with the Dolphins up 14–0 with only 2:53 left, the game suddenly turned interesting. With Miami going for the nail-in-the-coffin field goal, a bad snap turned into a nightmare. The Dolphins kicker Garo Yepremian picked up the loose ball, ran to his right, tried to throw it, and ended up fumbling. One of the Washington defensive backs, Mike Bass, picked up the ball and ran for a touchdown. Instead of a 17–0 game, it was suddenly 14–7.

The Yepremian blooper remains one of the most famous plays in football history, a source of comedy more than forty years later. At the time, though, it was anything but funny to Dolphins fans.

Washington got the ball back for one last chance with 1:14 left. At their own 30-yard line, Kilmer threw two incomplete passes and then one for a 4-yard loss. Faced with fourth and 14 from his own 26, Kilmer dropped back and, with his sights set on tying the game, couldn't escape the Miami pass rush and was sacked.

Game over.

The score looked closer than the game had felt, but that wasn't what people were talking about. The Dolphins were 17-0, completing the ultimate quest in sports. They had withstood the pressure of the un-defeated season, and Shula, the coach of the mighty Colts when the Jets had pulled off the greatest upset in football history in Super Bowl III, and the coach of the previous season's Dolphins team that had lost to the Cowboys in the Super Bowl, had finally earned his redemption.

Once it was over, the Dolphins knew they had ac-complished the most special feat a team could: They won all their games, and after only six years in exis-tence, had won the Super Bowl. No expansion team since the NFL had formed in the 1920s had won a title faster.

The next year, the Dolphins beat the 49ers and won their first game of the season, making it eighteen straight wins, but the Raiders beat them the following week, 12–7, and the historic streak finally came to an end. Miami would go on to win eleven of their final twelve games, avenge that loss to the Raiders by beat-ing them in the AFC title game, and win the Super Bowl for a second straight year, taking out Minnesota.

Going undefeated was the greatest achievement for Morris and Csonka and Morrall and the rest. No NFL team has done it since, but winning the next year proved that the Dolphins weren't just lucky. They were a legitimate powerhouse in the NFL, a team that would be a force to be reckoned with for years to come. In later years, when a team would start the season 10-0, fans would wonder if the undefeated Dolphins would finally have some company and another team could match their success. Yet so far, all these years later, the unbeaten 1972 Dolphins remain a club of one.

SUPER BOWL VII
TOP TEN LIST

The '72 Dolphins dominated the NFL with two running backs, Larry Csonka and Mercury Morris, who ran through defenses. Here is a list of the best running backs of all time. (Note that "best" doesn't always mean "has gained the most yards.")

1. Emmitt Smith, 1990–2004 (Dallas Cowboys, Arizona Cardinals): Three Super Bowl titles and NFL's all-time leading rusher with 18,355 yards.
2. Jim Brown, 1956–1965 (Cleveland Browns): He retired in 1965 as the all-time leading rusher; although he played only ten seasons and currently ranks ninth all-time in rushing yards, some maintain he was the best ever.
3. Barry Sanders, 1989–1998 (Detroit Lions): Electric, unpredictable, fast, and could change

direction on the run better than anyone. Gained 2,053 yards in 1997 season.

4. Eric Dickerson, 1983–1993 (Los Angeles Rams, Indianapolis Colts, Los Angeles Raiders, Atlanta Falcons): Tall, fast, and ran with power. Gained a record 2,105 yards in 1984.

5. Earl Campbell, 1978–1985 (Houston Oilers, New Orleans Saints): He attacked defenses, running over and through tacklers. Unfortunately his punishing style led to injuries and a career that was disappointingly short.

6. Tony Dorsett, 1977–1989 (Dallas Cowboys, Denver Broncos): Super-fast, slashing, almost elegant as he danced though the backfield. Scored on a 99-yard touchdown run in 1980.

7. Adrian Peterson, 2007–present (Minnesota Vikings): Called "All-Day" for his nonstop style.

8. Walter Payton, 1975–1987 (Chicago Bears): Retired as the NFL's all-time leading rusher (16,726 yards, which, to this day, trails only Emmitt Smith's total).

9. O. J. Simpson, 1969–1979 (Buffalo Bills, San Francisco 49ers): "The Juice." First man to rush

for 2,000 yards in a single season (1973).

10. Terrell Davis, 1995–2001 (Denver Broncos): Another fantastic career sadly shortened by injuries. Gained 2,008 yards and scored 21 touchdowns in 1998, leading the Broncos to a Super Bowl win.

SUPER BOWL X
THE BEST YET

PITTSBURGH STEELERS VS.
DALLAS COWBOYS

The year 1976 was one of anniversaries. The United States turned two hundred years old, and around the country, celebrations were held in recognition of America's independence from England. The Super Bowl turned ten years old, and ever since that day in Los Angeles a decade earlier when the Packers beat the Chiefs, the Big Game had been getting bigger and more popular. With family and friends coming together in living rooms across the country to watch, Super Bowl Sunday was quickly becoming an unofficial holiday.

There was one problem: the Big Game had never

really enjoyed a *great* game. There were great teams, like Lombardi's Packers and the undefeated Dolphins of '72. There were certainly great players, like Joe Namath, Bart Starr, and Fran Tarkenton.

What had been missing, though, was a combination of great teams and great players, the recipe for a classic no one would ever forget. Disappointingly, the Super Bowls thus far had been either blowouts, like when the Packers destroyed both the Chiefs and the Raiders in the first two Super Bowls, or sluggish, sloppy games, like when Miami beat Washington to go undefeated. America was hungry for a Super Bowl it would be talking about for years.

Super Bowl X finally provided that game. This one had everything. It had the Dallas Cowboys, a team that had not only appeared in two of the first nine Super Bowls, but had also played in one of the most famous games in football history, the 1967 NFL Championship against Green Bay. That game had been nicknamed the "Ice Bowl" because the wind-chill temperatures at game time were—get this—49 degrees BELOW ZERO.

The Cowboys lost that classic game 21–17, but they

had begun to capture the country's imagination as the popularity of football exploded.

By 1976, Dallas was on national TV all the time, so no matter where you lived, the Cowboys were on TV. Plus, they were consistently good, season after season. And the Cowboys were the first team to have cheerleaders, which made them glamorous and appealing to fans for a whole different reason.

These Cowboys also had their share of star players, starting with quarterback Roger Staubach, the Heisman Trophy winner from Navy, who could throw and scramble, and did the one thing that made opposing fans shake in their boots: He never gave up. Staubach was legendary for his ability to come back late in games and break the other team's hearts, like he'd done in Minnesota weeks earlier, in the famous "Hail Mary" game that knocked the Vikings—who had lost to the Steelers in the Super Bowl the year before—out of the playoffs. Minnesota had finished the season with a 12-2 record. They boasted one of the best defenses in the game, the famed "Purple People Eaters."

The classic game was played in frosty Minneapolis.

The temperature was 25 degrees. The Cowboys, trailing 14–10, took possession of the ball deep in their own territory with less than two minutes to play. The Vikings appeared to be on their way to another NFC Championship Game. Until . . .

Until Staubach said a Hail Mary and launched a 50-yard pass toward the end zone with just seconds left to play. Cowboys receiver Drew Pearson somehow caught the ball right up against the sideline at the 5-yard line, with his back to the end zone. He then turned and scored. Staubach's call for a miracle had been answered. Final score: Dallas 17, Minnesota 14.

Now, the "Purple People Eaters" was definitely a great moniker, but the Cowboys also had cool nicknames. They had a linebacker called Thomas "Hollywood" Henderson, a wide receiver named "Golden" Richards, and a future Hall of Fame defensive end known as Ed "Too Tall" Jones, because he was six foot nine. And the Cowboys' defense was good enough to have earned their own nickname: the Doomsday Defense.

But the Cowboys were only one half of Super Bowl X. Their opponents that day were the Pittsburgh Steelers. The Steelers were the defending champions, after all, having beaten the Vikings 16–6 in Super Bowl IX. The Steelers had been building a power-house for the past few seasons and now, along with Oakland and Miami, were among the upper echelon of the AFC. Dallas may have had the great Staubach, but Pittsburgh had rocket-armed Hall-of-Famer-to-be Terry Bradshaw at quarterback. They had one of the great running games thanks to another future Hall of Famer, Franco Harris, and his blocking back, Rocky Bleier. And they had not one but two future Hall of Fame receivers in John Stallworth and Lynn Swann. On the way to a 12-2 season, Pittsburgh had scored 373 points—an average of almost twenty-seven per game.

Despite their amazing talent on offense, the Steelers were actually best known for one thing: defense! The Steelers' defense had its own cool nickname—"The Steel Curtain"—and just like the offensive unit, it featured four future Hall of Fame players. It was arguably the most dominant defensive group ever assembled. There was lineman "Mean" Joe Greene, and line-backer Jack Lambert, one of the hardest-hitters ever. Lambert was missing his front teeth, which made him look like he had fangs. There was safety Mel Blount, a four-time All Pro and one of the best cornerbacks that football had ever seen, along with outside linebacker Jack Ham, who was unstoppable when chasing down the football. The Steelers in 1975 gave up 162 points, an average of just 11.5 per game.

So now it was Steelers-Cowboys, the matchup football fans everywhere wanted, the best of the AFC versus the best of the NFC.

The weather in Miami was perfect on January 18, 1976. Both teams wore commemorative bicentennial patches on their uniforms. The Steelers wore their menacing black and gold, the Cowboys their traditional silver and white with a blue star. Staubach versus the Steel Curtain, Bradshaw against the Doomsday Defense.

Dallas struck first, when Staubach hit Drew Pearson with a 29-yard touchdown. But the Steelers didn't waste time striking back. On the next possession, Lynn Swann leapt over the Cowboys defensive back Mark Washington on the sideline for a great catch that put the Steelers at the Dallas 16-yard line. From there, it was an easy score that tied the game at 7–7 in the first quarter.

Swann wasn't even supposed to play that day. He had been suffering from the effects of a concussion, so that even if he did play, he was not expected to be effective. The Cowboys had tried to scare Swann, saying before the game that they planned on hitting him so hard his sore head would definitely feel it.

But Swann played, and boy did he play, making the play of the game, one of the greatest, most acrobatic catches in Super Bowl history, getting tangled with Washington, falling down to the turf, yet keeping his eye on the ball. Unfortunately, the drive ended without a score for the Steelers, but to this day, the play remains one of the most memorable NFL moments of all time.

Soon the Steel Curtain began beating up Staubach, hitting him from all sides. Yet the Doomsday Defense held its own as the two defenses began to dominate.

Dallas led 10–7 entering the fourth quarter. That's when the Steelers turned things up. First, early in the fourth quarter, they blocked a punt for a safety (2 points) and then added two field goals for a 15–10 lead.

Then, with the Cowboy blitz on, Bradshaw got walloped by two Dallas defenders—so hard that they knocked him out of the game—but not before he had released the ball, which soared into the air . . . and

Swann did it again, catching a 64-yard touchdown pass to make it 21–10 (the Steelers kicker missed the extra point). Bradshaw never even saw the play—it was only when he returned to the locker room that he was told he had thrown for a touchdown.

Suddenly, the Super Bowl looked like it might turn into yet another blowout. Staubach, however, scrambling, running, desperate to escape the Steel Curtain, did what he did best: He refused to quit. He drove the Cowboys down the field before throwing a touchdown to cut the lead to 21–17. Time was running out, yet if Dallas could get the ball back, maybe Staubach had another miracle in him . . .

The Doomsday Defense did its job and held the Steelers' offense in check, giving the Cowboys one last chance. With three seconds left, enough for one desperate last shot, Staubach drove the Cowboys to midfield. He threw to Drew Pearson, just like he had in the Hail Mary game against Minnesota. Fans everywhere held their breath. But this time, there were three Steelers surrounding Pearson. The ball was tipped and intercepted in the end zone.

The game was over. The Steelers were victorious, winning their second straight Super Bowl. Swann, who had made multiple acrobatic catches, was named Most Valuable Player. Staubach had been sacked seven times and thrown three interceptions. In the end, it was the defense, the Steel Curtain, that had made the difference.

The game was not only the classic that the Super Bowl had previously lacked, it also solidified the Big Game itself as an American tradition, something Americans would flock to, either by trying to go to the game or by setting up in front of the TV on Super Bowl Sunday, hoping each game would be as memorable a show as the one put on by Pittsburgh and Dallas.

SUPER BOWL X
TOP TEN LIST

Lynn Swann was one of the most acrobatic wide receivers in history. He dominated Super Bowl X, but it took him years to finally be admitted into the Pro Football Hall of Fame. Over time, the game would become dominated by quarterbacks and passing. Here is a list of the game's greatest pass catchers. (Again, note that "best" doesn't necessarily mean "has the most catches.")

1. Jerry Rice, 1985–2004 (San Francisco 49ers, Oakland Raiders, Seattle Seahawks): Scored 197 touchdowns and caught 1,549 passes for 22,895 yards—*all* of which are NFL records. Also a three-time Super Bowl champ. Hard to rank anyone ahead of him.

2. Randy Moss, 1998–2012 (Minnesota Vikings, Oakland Raiders, New England Patriots, Tennessee Titans, San Francisco 49ers): The best

deep threat ever to play. Scored 156 touchdowns, including 23 in 2007.

3. Michael Irvin, 1988–1999 (Dallas Cowboys): Known simply as "The Playmaker." A three-time Super Bowl champ who retired with 11,904 yards receiving.

4. Calvin Johnson, 2007–present (Detroit Lions): Called "Megatron" for his superhuman skills, he is likely the best all-around athlete on this list. Has gained 10,405 yards in seven seasons, including an NFL-record 1,964 in 2012.

5. Rob Gronkowski, 2010–present (New England Patriots): Caught 17 touchdowns as a tight end in 2011. His rare combination of size and speed make him a game changer.

6. Terrell Owens, 1996–2010 (San Francisco 49ers, Philadelphia Eagles, Dallas Cowboys, Buffalo Bills, Cincinnati Bengals): Caught 1,078 receptions for 15,934 yards and 153 touchdowns, ranking him second all-time in receiving yards, and third in receiving touchdowns. Known for his flashy touchdown celebrations and knack for racking up fines and penalties.

7. Cris Carter, 1987–2002 (Philadelphia Eagles,

Minnesota Vikings, Miami Dolphins): Before trading him, Buddy Ryan once famously criticized Carter, "All he does is catch touchdown passes." The Vikings were fine with that, along with Carter's 1,101 total passes caught.

8. Tony Gonzalez, 1997–2013 (Kansas City Chiefs, Atlanta Falcons): He brought speed to the tight end position and recorded 1,325 career receptions, the most all-time for a tight end and second among all receivers.

9. Fred Biletnikoff, 1965–1978 (Oakland Raiders): His hands were so good they named an award after him in college football. This Super Bowl XI MVP became a Hall of Famer in 1988.

10. Andre Reed, 1985–2000 (Buffalo Bills, Washington): Finished his career with 951 receptions, 13,198 receiving yards, and four Super Bowl appearances.

SUPER BOWL XI
THE BAD GUYS WIN

~~~~~~

OAKLAND RAIDERS VS.
MINNESOTA VIKINGS

I t was in Pasadena, on January 9, 1977, where the Oakland Raiders or Minnesota Vikings would finally be one of the few teams good enough to win the last game of the season and call themselves Super Bowl champions. It would be a long time coming for either team.

From the time in 1966 when the old American Football League and National Football League played the first Super Bowl, to when the two rival leagues merged in 1970, the Raiders had been so close to the championship they could practically touch the trophy—

except for one big problem: another team was always holding it after the final whistle.

In the three seasons between 1967 and 1969, the Raiders were awesome. Their record during those seasons was 37-4-1. Yet they lost Super Bowl II 33–14 to the Green Bay Packers, the next year's AFL title game 27–23 to the New York Jets (who then won Super Bowl III), and then *next* year's AFL title game to Kansas City. Like the Jets before them, the Chiefs beat the Raiders and then won the Super Bowl. Three dominant seasons. Nothing to show for it.

On it went.

1972: A heartbreaking 13–7 loss to Pittsburgh in the AFC Divisional Playoff.

1973: The Raiders lost 27–10 to Miami in the AFC Championship Game. The Dolphins went on to win the Super Bowl.

1974: The Raiders lost 24–13 to Pittsburgh in the AFC Championship Game. The Steelers went on to win the Super Bowl.

1975: The Raiders lost 16–10 to Pittsburgh, yet again in the AFC Championship. The Steelers, predictably, went on to win their second Super Bowl.

It wasn't losing, however, that defined the Oakland Raiders in those days. It was toughness and dishing it out. They were the bad boys of the NFL, the team that lived up to their nickname. Jack Tatum was one of the meanest safeties in the history of the game. His partner at safety, George Atkinson, wasn't far behind. Linebacker Ted "The Stork" Hendricks was tall and ferocious when chasing quarterbacks, Willie Brown was an undrafted shutdown cornerback who captained the Raider defense for a decade, and John "Tooz" Matuszak was a high-energy defensive lineman who once competed in a World's Strongest Man competition.

The Raiders seemed to play with a chip on their shoulders, forever daring opposing teams to knock it off. They were a tough football team in a tough city—a city overshadowed by their more glamorous neighbor, San Francisco. They had been founded in 1960 by Al Davis, a brash owner who was as unpopular in the NFL as his bad-boy team. Yet neither seemed to care—and the fans of Oakland embraced the Raiders for it.

The Raiders relished the roles of outcasts and underdogs. If the rest of the league thought a player couldn't do the job, the Raiders would give him a chance to prove he could. If the in-crowd of the NFL didn't like your looks because you had long hair and a scraggly beard, the Raiders made you feel right at home. In short, there was pretty, and then there were the Raiders.

Oakland wasn't just a collection of bullies, though. They were a squad bursting with talent, led by a scrambling left-handed quarterback from Alabama, Ken "The Snake" Stabler. Their top two receivers, Dave Casper and Fred Biletnikoff, were tough, reliable, and blessed with soft hands. (Biletnikoff was not only a Hall of Famer, but he was so good that to this day college football honors the best wide receiver in the game each season with the Biletnikoff Award.) The speedy Cliff Branch, meanwhile, was one of the best deep threats in the league. Clarence Davis, Pete Banaszak and Mark van Eeghen formed a talented trio running the ball behind an offensive line that featured two future Hall of Famers: Art Shell and Gene Upshaw.

The Raiders represented their city, body and soul, as few others would in the history of the game. The defense didn't have a memorable nickname for their ferocious ways, like Denver's Orange Crush or Pittsburgh's Steel Curtain. The name "Oakland" was intimidation enough.

They went 13-1 in the regular season, beating the defending champion Steelers in the first game. In Week 4, they went to up to Schaefer Stadium and were destroyed 48–17 by a young, rapidly improving New England team in their only loss of the season. No other team would score 30 points on the Raiders' defense all season.

After losing to the Patriots, the Raiders won ten straight to finish the season, and the reward was a play-off rematch against the Patriots, this time in Oakland. The Raiders were on their way to losing again to New England, down 21–17 in the final minutes, facing a third down and 17, when fate intervened.

Stabler, facing a third down and 18 with just over a minute left to play, threw an incomplete pass, and Patriots fans thought that would be the end of the Raiders' chances. Yet New England defensive end Ray "Sugar Bear" Hamilton was called for roughing the passer. That gave the Raiders new life and Stabler took advantage, scoring the winning touchdown himself with just ten seconds remaining.

The AFC Championship Game, not surprisingly, pitted the Raiders against the Steelers for the third consecutive season. This time, however, proved to be sweet revenge for Oakland, an easy 24–7 win. The Raiders were back in the Super Bowl.

Their opponents, the Minnesota Vikings, may have been the only team in the world that could say they were as hungry to win, or as hungry to erase the taste of losing time and time again, as the Raiders.

Amazingly, out of the ten Super Bowls played up to this point, the Vikings had played in three—and lost each of them. In fact, the Vikings hadn't just lost, they had gotten thumped.

Hard.

Super Bowl IV: Chiefs 23, Vikings 7
Super Bowl VIII: Dolphins 24, Vikings 7
Super Bowl IX: Steelers 16, Vikings 6

Three Super Bowls, only 20 points scored combined.

And that is what's so weird about sports and losing, because nobody could ever have called the Vikings losers. Their quarterback, Fran Tarkenton, was one of the most exciting players in the game to watch, a future Hall of Famer who could run as well as he could pass. Chuck Foreman was a hard-nosed running back who rushed for more than 1,000 yards in three consecutive seasons (which was much harder to accomplish in a fourteen-game schedule), and deep threat receiver Sammy White was terrific. The defensive line was loaded with Pro Bowlers, led by future Hall of Famers Alan Page and Carl Eller. They were so good that they earned what may have been the best nickname of them all, the "Purple People Eaters."

In 1976, the Vikings were a little older, yet they still went 11-2-1—including wins against Pittsburgh and Miami. In the playoffs they destroyed Washington and the Los Angeles Rams to—once more—reach the Super Bowl.

Now one of these teams, Oakland or Minnesota, would finally taste Super Bowl victory.

Unfortunately, the game felt over by halftime, with the Raiders leading 16–0. Nothing the Vikings did worked. The lead soon swelled to 26–7. The Purple

People Eaters were getting run over on the ground by Clarence Davis and slashed through the air by Stabler and Biletnikoff. The Vikings couldn't move the ball in response.

The final score was 32–14. The Raiders were too focused, too hungry, too close to finally tasting victory this time to be denied. The team picked up head coach John Madden (yes, the Madden who would later be immortalized thanks to the Madden NFL video game) and carried him back to the locker room on their shoulders. Like Lynn Swann the year before against Dallas, a wide receiver won the MVP Award. This time, it was Biletnikoff.

The lasting image of the game, fittingly, was one of the Raiders' signature bone-crushing hits. Sammy White had run over the middle—into Jack Tatum territory—and Tatum hit White so hard that White's helmet came off. The helmet flew to the left while the chin strap went right, and White went down, Tatum standing over him like a conqueror.

Super Bowl XI would be like many important Super Bowls, a lousy game with a significant outcome. The Vikings would become the first team in history to lose four Super Bowls. What was worse was that no one knew it then, but 1977 would be the last time Minnesota would play for a championship to this day. The Vikings left the field that afternoon and in nearly forty years have never found their way back to the Super Bowl.

Meanwhile, after having come so close for so many years, the Raiders were finally crowned champions. The victory soothed the wounds of losing all those years. The people of Oakland were champions, and the Raiders were on their way to becoming a legendary NFL team, for beating the Vikings was just the start. They would win the Super Bowl again in 1980 and a third time in 1983.

SUPER BOWL XI
TOP TEN LIST

Football is supposed to be a game of rules, but that doesn't stop guys from kicking, spitting, biting, hitting after the whistle, or doing just about anything when they lose their tempers. Some guys don't even need to get mad to play dirty or try to purposely injure other players. Here is a list of ten guys who never thought twice about breaking the rules.

1. Lyle Alzado, defensive end, 1971–1985 (Denver Broncos, Cleveland Browns, Los Angeles Raiders): Known for his short temper and for throwing (opponents') helmets.
2. Jack Tatum, safety, 1971–1980 (Oakland Raiders, Houston Oilers): He earned the nickname "The Assassin" by launching himself at receivers.
3. Conrad Dobler, guard, 1972–1981 (St. Louis

Cardinals, New Orleans Saints, Buffalo Bills):
He used anything and everything to attack
defensive linemen, including his teeth and his
fists.

4. Fred Williamson, cornerback, 1960–1967
(Pittsburgh Steelers, Oakland Raiders, Kansas
City Chiefs): Nicknamed "The Hammer" for good
reason—he liked to hit receivers in the head with
his arms. Hard.

5. Bill Romanowski, linebacker, 1988–2003 (San
Francisco 49ers, Philadelphia Eagles, Denver
Broncos, Oakland Raiders): He earned his
reputation by, among other things, kicking one
player in the head and spitting in the face of
another. Once beat up one of his own teammates!

6. Ndamukong Suh, defensive tackle, 2010–present
(Detroit Lions, Miami Dolphins): One of the most
dominant players in the game today is also one
of the most fined and penalized, most notably
for kicking a quarterback in the groin and for
stomping on another player who was already on
the ground.

7. James Harrison, linebacker, 2002–2014

(Pittsburgh Steelers, Cincinnati Bengals): When the NFL changed its rules to eliminate hits to the head, Harrison racked up fines like they were parking tickets.

8. Steve Wisniewski, guard, 1989–2001 (Los Angeles / Oakland Raiders): He specialized in "cut blocking," a technique used to take out players by hitting them in the knees.

9. Richie Incognito, center, 2006–present (St. Louis Rams, Miami Dolphins, Buffalo Bills): Voted the NFL's Dirtiest Player . . . a full four years *before* he was suspended for half of the 2013 season for bullying a member of his own team.

10. Kevin Gogan, guard, 1987–2000 (Dallas Cowboys, Los Angeles / Oakland Raiders, San Francisco 49ers, Miami Dolphins, San Diego Chargers): Nicknamed "Big Nasty." Need I say more?

SECOND DOWN

SUPER BOWL XIII
THE REMATCH,
PART I

PITTSBURGH STEELERS VS. DALLAS COWBOYS

n the 1970s there were, without a doubt, two signature teams that dominated the NFL: the Dallas Cowboys and Pittsburgh Steelers. Not only had the Cowboys and Steelers played the most exciting and competitive Super Bowl in league history up to that point, in Super Bowl X, but they continued to be the teams to beat in the NFC and AFC. The Cowboys were now routinely known as "America's Team," ever since an announcer coined the term in

1978, saying, "They appear on television so often that their faces are as familiar to the public as presidents and movie stars." Such fame caused most fans to either love Dallas or hate them, but because they were on TV around the country every week, you could not ignore them.

The Steelers were just good, so good that they made the playoffs season after season and many of their players became household names. One was the defensive end "Mean" Joe Greene, who became famous for appearing in a Coca-Cola commercial in which he limps down a stadium tunnel, clearly injured, and then a kid hands him a bottle of Coke. Mean Joe, the meanest, toughest player in the league, downs the soda, cracks a smile, and says, "Hey kid, catch!" and tosses the kid his jersey. In those days, there weren't hundreds of channels to choose from. There were just three network channels—so everyone across America saw that commercial. And loved it.

After the epic Super Bowl the two teams had played three years earlier, the football world wanted a rematch. The Steelers and Cowboys had each won two Super Bowls by this point. In fact, the Cowboys had already appeared in four of the eight Super Bowls in the decade, while the Steelers had appeared in two. When they'd met in Super Bowl X, the Steelers had been the defending champions, and now heading into Super Bowl XIII, the Cowboys were defending the Lombardi Trophy they had won the year before by beating Denver.

The two teams' players were equally iconic. Even if you weren't a Cowboys fan, you knew Randy White, Ed "Too Tall" Jones, and "Hollywood" Henderson on defense. You knew the image of coach Tom Landry on the sidelines in his fedora hat, dress coat and tie. And of course you recognized the star-studded offense, led by quarterback Roger Staubach. Staubach was playing his fourteenth season, was a fixture in the playoffs, had won a Heisman Trophy, and had earned the cool nickname "Captain Comeback." And now the Cowboys had a new star, having won Super Bowl XII with their latest weapon, the wondrous running back from the University of Pittsburgh, Tony Dorsett.

The Steelers, meanwhile, still rode on the collective backs of their legendary defense, the Steel Curtain, and the dynamic offensive foursome of quarterback Terry Bradshaw, running back Franco Harris, and wide receivers Lynn Swann and John Stallworth.

They were coached by the meticulous Chuck Noll, as quiet and introverted off the field as he was demanding on it.

After a disappointing 9-5 record and a divisional playoff loss to the Broncos in 1977, the '78 Steelers brought football greatness back to Pittsburgh. That year, the NFL expanded the season from fourteen to sixteen games and Pittsburgh went 14-2. Their defense was number one in the league again. They started the season with seven straight wins. In the playoffs, they destroyed Denver and Houston by a combined score of 67–15 to reach the Super Bowl yet again.

The Cowboys were nearly as good, with the top-ranked offense and the third-ranked defense. Dorsett had a Pro Bowl season, rushing for 1,325 yards and 7 touchdowns. Staubach didn't have a single standout receiver, but he did have many dependable weapons. Rookie Tony Hill had downfield speed and had caught 46 passes for 823 yards. Two other players, Preston Pearson and Drew Pearson (not related to each other), also caught at least 40 passes, while Dorsett had 37 receptions. In short, they had plenty of firepower on offense to go with their Doomsday Defense.

The Cowboys had dominated the Rams 28–0 in

the NFC title game to earn the opportunity they had waited two years for: a Super Bowl rematch with the Steelers.

The game was played in Miami, the same site as their first meeting, and like that first meeting, Dallas went up early, this time 14–7. Again, the Pittsburgh wide receivers were the difference-makers. Lynn Swann caught 7 passes for 124 yards and John Stallworth caught 3, but they were game-breakers, totaling 115 yards, including a 75-yard strike from Bradshaw that tied the game at 14. Pittsburgh led 21–14 at the half.

In the third quarter, with the Steelers still up by a touchdown, the Cowboys were driving down the field, determined to put points on the scoreboard. As they neared the end zone, Dallas's veteran tight end Jackie Smith had an opportunity to help his team tie the game.

Jackie Smith had played for the St. Louis Cardinals for fifteen years (this was before the Cardinals moved to Arizona, and before the Rams moved from Los Angeles to fill the gap left by the Cardinals). Smith had been one of the best in the game, catching more than 40 passes in seven different seasons and playing in 121 straight games. Then he was told by doctors that he was risking his life playing football. They told him the wrong hit at the wrong time might kill him or paralyze him.

So, in 1977, Jackie Smith retired. He left the game with 7,918 receiving yards, the most ever (for a few years, at least) among tight ends. He ended up opening and working at a restaurant that he named "Jackie's Place."

However, while the Cowboys were making their playoff run, their regular tight end, Jay Saldi, was injured. Dallas needed a replacement, so they called Jackie Smith and asked him to come out of retirement. In all those years playing with the Cardinals, Smith had only been to the playoffs twice and hadn't won a game either time. He accepted the offer.

Now, here he was, the oldest man on the field at age thirty-eight, finally at the Super Bowl, the biggest game of his life. It was third down and 3 to go from the Steelers' 10. The Cowboys were in a running formation, a two-tight-end set, just a few yards away from a first down. The Steelers were expecting Dorsett to run the ball, but Staubach chose to drop back and pass.

Quietly, Smith slipped past the line of scrimmage and into the end zone, wide open.

Staubach saw him. And threw.

Smith saw the ball, then stumbled slightly.

On the sidelines, Landry raised his hands to signal "touchdown." Everyone watching the play thought the same thing.

But Smith dropped the pass.

And Landry quickly dropped his hands, wincing at the colossal mistake.

To this day, it remains the worst drop in Super Bowl history. And it was heartbreaking for everyone hoping to see Smith end his career on a high note.

The Cowboys instead settled for a field goal to cut the lead to 21–17.

Then, aided by two controversial penalties, including a debatable pass interference call against Dallas that put the Steelers at the Cowboys' 23-yard line, Pittsburgh scored 2 more touchdowns to open a commanding 35–17 lead. With only seven minutes left in the game, the Steelers appeared to be on the verge of victory.

But Captain Comeback and the rest of the Cowboys refused to give up. On their next drive, it took the

Cowboys just eight plays to move the ball 89 yards down the field and into the end zone, cutting the Pittsburgh lead to 11.

With just over two minutes remaining, the Cowboys were in desperation mode. It was time to pull out all the stops—and indeed they did, successfully recovering an onside kick on their own 48-yard line. Two 20-yard catches from Drew Pearson kept the momentum going, and Dallas scored another touchdown to cut the lead to 35–31.

With only twenty-six seconds left on the clock, the Cowboys had to rely on a miracle: recovering yet another onside kick. One last shot to complete an incredible comeback.

But the ball ended up in the hands of Rocky Bleier, the Steelers' dependable fullback, and Pittsburgh ran out the clock. The Steelers won the game—their third Super Bowl victory in five years.

For the rest of his life, Jackie Smith would be haunted by his infamous drop and the 4 points that could've been the difference. He retired again after the game.

No one could have known it at the time, but Tom Landry's Cowboys would never reach another Super

Bowl. Staubach, who ran for so many first downs, threw for so many touchdowns, and took so many hits, suffered a concussion in a 21–19 playoff loss the following season to the Rams. It would be Staubach's final game in the NFL. He, too, chose to retire.

Even without Staubach, the Cowboys were still contenders. Former backup quarterback Danny White took over for Staubach, and the Cowboys reached the NFC title game each of the next three years, only to be beaten by Philadelphia, then San Francisco, and finally Washington.

The Cowboys, the NFC team of the 1970s, would be replaced by other teams in the 1980s. Finally, after being the only coach in Cowboys history, Landry was fired in 1988.

The Cowboys wouldn't reach the Super Bowl again until 1993.

After beating the Cowboys, the Steelers won the Super Bowl again the next year, handily beating the Rams 31–19. It was their fourth Super Bowl in four tries, clearly making Pittsburgh the team of the decade. Pittsburgh was the first team in history to win four Super Bowls. They started the decade as a team that hadn't reached the playoffs since 1947 and ended it having completely rewritten their history. The Steelers were now one of the greatest franchises in the league.

After the Steelers beat the Rams in Super Bowl XIV, the dynasty died, having given way to age and injury, as they all eventually do. Bradshaw played four more seasons, injured his elbow, and never fully recovered. Franco Harris would finish his career with Seattle, a shell of the once-great running back he had been. One by one, the pieces would fade away, including Noll, who was replaced in 1992.

The Steelers' absence from the Super Bowl would last fifteen years, when, fittingly, a whole new generation of players would come face to face with an old foe: the Dallas Cowboys.

Still, no matter how many seasons passed, no one could ever forget the Steel Curtain, or the pain of Jackie Smith's drop, or the never-say-die spirit of the Dallas Cowboys, the team that lost to Pittsburgh twice in the Super Bowl, but gave fans first a classic and then a rematch to remember.

SUPER BOWL XIII
TOP TEN LIST

Super Bowl XIII played host to a contest between two of the greatest defenses of all time, but it was also a game featuring two of the greatest defense nicknames ever: the Steel Curtain and the Doomsday Defense. Almost all of the great defenses in NFL history (with the exception of the 2000 Baltimore Ravens) have had great, unforgettable nicknames. Here is a list of the very best.

1. The Purple People Eaters (Minnesota Vikings, 1970–1977)
2. The Steel Curtain (Pittsburgh Steelers, 1972–1980)
3. The Doomsday Defense (Dallas Cowboys, 1970–1980)
4. The Legion of Boom (Seattle Seahawks [specifically the secondary], 2013–present)
5. Big Blue Wrecking Crew (New York Giants, 1985–1991)

6. Fearsome Foursome (Los Angeles Rams, 1960s)
7. No-Name Defense (Miami Dolphins, 1970s)
8. New York Sack Exchange (New York Jets, 1980s)
9. Orange Crush (Denver Broncos, 1970s)
10. The '85 Bears (The name speaks for itself. Not much of a nickname, but they were too good not to include.)

SUPER BOWL XVI
THE DAWN OF
A DYNASTY

SAN FRANCISCO 49ERS VS.
CINCINNATI BENGALS

People don't like change, whether it's food or a favorite shirt or football. *Especially* football.

Since the earliest roots of the game, football was played one way:

First down: run the football.

Second down: run the football.

Third down: pass when you need a lot of yards, run when you need only a few.

Fourth down: punt or kick a field goal.

Football used to be all about the power running

game. Running back Jim Brown of the Cleveland Browns of the 1950s and 1960s is still considered by some to be the greatest player of all time, even though he is no longer the game's all-time leading rusher. In the 1970s, the sport was dominated by stars like O. J. Simpson, Franco Harris, Tony Dorsett, and Larry Csonka. A big-time running attack—that was the way the game had always been played.

Until Bill Walsh came along and decided to reinvent the game, to be the one to say, "Maybe that's the way it's always been done, but let's try it this way." And professional football would never be the same.

Walsh, born and raised in Northern California, attended San Jose State University. In 1966, at the age of thirty-seven, Walsh entered professional football as the running backs coach for the Oakland Raiders, and went on to become the wide receivers coach for the AFL's Cincinnati Bengals. His mind was always curious, always ready to push boundaries, never prepared to simply follow tradition. The AFL was more of a passing league than the NFL, and Walsh began thinking of newer, innovative ways to create an offense. There were other architects of the passing game, but for most of them, from Sid Gillman in San Diego to his understudy, Don Coryell (who would later bring a pass-happy offense of his own to the NFL, known as "Air Coryell"), the emphasis was on "stretching the field," throwing deep bombs to speedy wide receivers who put immense pressure on the cornerbacks.

Walsh, however, recognized a flaw in this system: A quarterback had to have a strong arm to be able to throw the ball 50 or 60 yards downfield. He wanted to create an offensive system for a quarterback whose arm wasn't as strong, and who played for a team that didn't have one of those power running backs to carry the load.

Walsh's first head coaching job was in college, at Stanford University. After two years, he was hired by the San Francisco 49ers, where he finally had an opportunity to put his theories to work in the NFL. The 49ers had been part of the NFL since 1950 and, in all that time, had never won a championship. They had come close in the early 1970s, but were beaten in the NFC title game by the Cowboys in 1971 and 1972.

In 1978, the year before Walsh took over as head coach, the 49ers finished with a record of 2-14, the worst record in the league. The 49ers, and their fans, were ready for a change.

In Walsh's first year with the team, 1979, they selected Joe Montana, a quarterback from Notre Dame, in the third round of the draft. Montana had led one of the most celebrated comebacks in college football history as a senior in the annual Cotton Bowl and had led Notre Dame to consecutive Top Ten finishes, yet he was considered anything but a sure bet in the NFL. In fact, because of his modest arm strength, Montana ended up being the fourth quarterback chosen in the draft. Yet Walsh thought Montana would be perfect for his system.

Montana sat on the bench for most of his rookie year, backing up Steve DeBerg. It wasn't until midway through his second season, 1980, that Montana took over the starting quarterback job for good. The team finished 6-10 that year, but Walsh recognized his new quarterback's improvement week after week.

The 49ers were developing some formidable weapons in addition to Montana, including the sure-handed wide receiver Dwight Clark and the speedy wide-out Freddie Solomon.

The young defense was terrific as well, and it only improved in 1981, when San Francisco drafted future Hall of Famer Ronnie Lott out of USC, who played cornerback at the time (he would later switch to safety). He instantly became a leader both in the locker room and on the field. The young talent was seemingly everywhere, so despite the 49ers' losing record, there was certainly reason for hope. Yet everything hinged on Walsh, his offensive system, and his quarterback.

1981 marked the year all three hit their stride. The 49ers went 13-3 that season, at times looking unstoppable. In the sixth game of the season, for instance, they crushed mighty Dallas 45–14, the same team that had beaten them 59–14 the year before.

The 49ers had surprised the entire league with Walsh's unique and potent offense. It was obvious that Walsh thought about football differently than other coaches. In his view, if the goal was to get 10 yards for a first down, what difference did it make if it came from the run or the pass?

Yes, passing was more risky: There was always a chance of an interception or a wasted down if the quarterback threw an incomplete pass, but Montana was perfectly suited for Walsh's short-yard passing game, with its emphasis on precision. While most teams typically had two or three players line up as receivers, Walsh would utilize four or even five. Before

Walsh came along and rocked the boat, teams would use their running backs to run and to block. But Walsh turned his running backs into receivers who could catch as well as run. Montana turned out to be the perfect quarterback for an offense that relied on touch and timing.

Montana was such an accurate passer, in fact, that the 49ers could consistently throw on first down for 5 yards, leaving the defense not knowing what to expect on second down—another throw or a run. Not knowing which option to cover, the defense left open the potential for either, increasing the chances that the 49ers would pick up a first down. Walsh and Montana left defenses feeling off-balance in a way they hadn't experienced before.

Walsh revolutionized the offensive side of the game in other ways, as well. With his pass-first offense, he also developed a new form of play that changed football: running after the catch. Prior to Walsh's time in the league, quarterbacks would typically throw the ball around 40 yards downfield to the receiver: It was like playing a game of catch with defenders trying to prevent the connection. Clearly, though, Walsh wasn't satisfied with the status quo. He drafted quick players who were difficult to tackle. This allowed Montana to throw a 5-yard pass to a receiver on the run, who could then run for 25 yards after the catch. Suddenly, a 5-yard gain turned into a 30-yard play. This tactic made Walsh's offense more efficient, because it was easier to catch a 5-yard pass than a 30-yarder, and more dangerous, because so many of his receivers could run after the catch, turning short plays into big ones.

The 1981 team's thirteen wins were the most in franchise history. San Francisco then went on to defeat the Giants in the divisional playoffs, propelling them to the NFC title game, where they would face the mighty Dallas Cowboys. So many ghosts surrounded this game.

But the 49ers, especially Montana, were confident. They knew from crushing the Cowboys earlier in the season that they could move the ball against the aging, fading Doomsday Defense. They also had home-field advantage. And most importantly, the 49ers felt they had been the best team all season, and were dead set on proving it.

What the team couldn't anticipate was how sloppy the field would be, or how sloppy the 49ers' offense would look playing on that field. The usually steady Montana threw three interceptions and the 49ers fumbled three more times. The Cowboys took advantage and, with only a few minutes left, took a 27–21 lead.

Down by 6 on their own 11-yard line with 4:54 left, San Francisco needed a touchdown to win. That's when Montana went to work, beginning the first chapter of being the cool customer under pressure that would become his trademark and earn him the nickname "Joe Cool."

Montana hit Solomon for a first down to get them out to the 23-yard line. Now, at least, they were out from the shadow of their own goal line. From there, the offense looked like the one fans had seen all season, driving past midfield, edging closer to the end zone. Short passes to Clark and to Solomon mixed with a Lenvil Elliott run had the Cowboys' defense backpedaling.

With fifty-eight seconds left to play, the 49ers had the ball at the Cowboys' 6-yard line.

Third down, three to go, from the 6. Walsh called a play known as "Sprint Right Option," in which Montana took the snap and ran to his right. Solomon was his intended target, but the defense had him well covered. Meanwhile, Clark ran into the end zone, then darted left, only to stop and run back to the right as he saw Montana drifting and drifting to his right, trying to find an open receiver.

Defensive end Ed "Too Tall" Jones, all six foot nine of him, was breathing down Montana's neck. The linebacker D. D. Lewis was chasing him, right along with the other defensive end, Larry Bethea. Faced with intense pressure from the defense, Montana had a split second to find an open man.

Montana floated a ball into the end zone. Everson Walls, the Cowboys cornerback who had already intercepted Montana twice, stood in the end zone and watched the ball float toward the back of the goal line. He positioned himself to make the interception. What he never saw coming was Clark jumping over him, reaching high, and clutching the ball with his fingertips for the touchdown!

Montana never even saw Clark catch the ball. Bethea had knocked him to the ground and out of bounds. But he heard the roar of the crowd. That was all the indication he needed. The 49ers had taken the lead.

The Cowboys had one final chance, but quarterback Danny White fumbled in the final seconds. The 49ers had won. They were going to the Super Bowl.

Too Tall Jones looked at Montana and said, "You just beat America's Team."

"Well," Montana said, "you can sit at home with the rest of America and watch the Super Bowl."

The Super Bowl was played in the Pontiac Silverdome outside of Detroit against another surprise team, the Cincinnati Bengals, the team Walsh once worked for as an assistant. Early on, the 49ers blazed away, taking a 20–0 lead at halftime, capitalizing on a couple of Bengals turnovers. At the time, it was the largest halftime lead in Super Bowl history. To many, the game appeared over already.

But not to the Bengals, who clawed back with a second-half rally, including a nine-play, 83-yard drive that concluded with a rushing touchdown by their MVP quarterback, Ken Anderson.

Each time Cincinnati was on the verge of making a serious comeback, though, the 49ers had an answer. On a particularly gut-wrenching drive, the Bengals threw for the end zone on third and goal at the 1-yard line. Led by linebacker Dan Bunz, San

Francisco famously stopped the Bengals' running back Charles Alexander at the goal line to keep a 20–7 lead.

Despite the disappointing conclusion to that drive, the Bengals defense came onto the field and held the 49ers to just 8 yards. Cincinnati got the ball back near midfield and took advantage of their excellent field position. They scored a touchdown when Anderson threw a 4-yard pass to his tight end, Dan Ross. Suddenly, the Bengals had cut the lead to 20–14.

Even so, the 49ers refused to budge. Due to a combination of defense and the offense taking time off the clock, San Francisco kept their lead, adding a pair of field goals to make the score 26–14. The Bengals had one more touchdown drive in them, but with only twenty seconds left on the clock, it was too little too late. The 49ers won their first Super Bowl 26–21.

The 49ers were champions who had transformed from losers into winners. They would go on to dominate the 1980s and become the "team of the decade." Three years after defeating the Bengals in Super Bowl XVI, the 49ers would win their second Super Bowl. Four years later they would win their third. The year after, they won their fourth. Thanks to Bill Walsh and to Pro Bowl players such as Montana, Clark, Lott, running back Roger Craig, offensive linemen Guy McIntyre and Randy Cross, receiver Jerry Rice, and pass rush specialist Charles Haley, the 49ers became a dynasty.

In light of its success, the Walsh-style offense was copied by coaches and teams around the league. A new type of offense had forever been established in the NFL—the "West Coast" offense. It was the ultimate compliment to a coach who was bold enough to try reinventing the game, and smart enough to actually succeed doing so.

SUPER BOWL XVI
TOP TEN LIST

ill Walsh and Joe Montana proved to be an unbeatable combination, and in football, the pairing of a great coach and a great quarterback is often the key to winning championships. Here is a list of the best quarterback-coach combinations in league history.

1. Joe Montana–Bill Walsh (San Francisco 49ers): Revolutionized the NFL in creating the West Coast offense. Won three Super Bowl titles.

2. Tom Brady–Bill Belichick (New England Patriots): Transformed the New England Patriots from a subpar team into a dynasty. Have won four Super Bowl titles together thus far.

3. Roger Staubach–Tom Landry (Dallas Cowboys): Catapulted the Cowboys to greatness, which led them to become known as "America's Team." Six Super Bowl appearances.

4. Terry Bradshaw–Chuck Noll (Pittsburgh Steelers): First team to win four Super Bowls.

5. Dan Fouts–Don Coryell (San Diego Chargers): Created arguably the most exciting passing attack ever, which earned the nickname "Air Coryell."

6. Brett Favre–Mike Holmgren (Green Bay Packers): Returned the Packers to their glory days. Two Super Bowl appearances and one victory.

7. Bart Starr–Vince Lombardi (Green Bay Packers): Turned the Packers into the first great dynasty in the Super Bowl era.

8. Jim Kelly–Marv Levy (Buffalo Bills): Four straight Super Bowl appearances from 1991 to 1994.

9. John Elway–Mike Shanahan (Denver Broncos): Led Denver to consecutive Super Bowl titles.

10. Fran Tarkenton–Bud Grant (Minnesota Vikings): Architects of Minnesota's glory years in the '70s.

SUPER BOWL XX
THE DEMOLITION

CHICAGO BEARS VS. NEW ENGLAND PATRIOTS

How good were the 1985 Chicago Bears on defense? They were so good they didn't even need a cool nickname, like the Steel Curtain or the Purple People Eaters. To this day, just saying "the '85 Bears" is a huge statement all by itself. No defense has ever been as dominant.

Yes, the Bears had a charismatic quarterback in Jim McMahon. Yes, they had a Hall of Fame running back in Walter "Sweetness" Payton and an Olympic-caliber sprinter at wide receiver in Willie Gault. Yet this team would become famous for one reason and one reason only: their dangerous defense. During the season, the offense and defense made headlines. They were a tough, cocky bunch of characters who gave crazy interviews. McMahon fought with the league commissioner, Pete Rozelle, over the very strict rules regarding—this is a true story—what kinds of headbands players could wear. The Bears players were so feisty they sometimes even fought with each other. They also made a famously funny music video, "The Super Bowl Shuffle." On the field, the 1985 Chicago Bears were simply the best at taking an offense and crushing them. They were characters, but their defense defined them.

The NFC was crowded in the 1980s—season after season, many talented teams contended for the league championship. San Francisco would become the premiere team of the decade, but the Giants, Washington, the Los Angeles Rams (before they moved to St. Louis), and, of course, the Dallas Cowboys, were also consistently in the picture.

The Bears had been a good team in 1984, but they weren't yet great. They were shut out 23–0 by the 49ers in the NFC Championship Game. Then in 1985, the Bears became dominant on the shoulders of their defense.

The Bears were from the tough city of Chicago, which meant they were expected to be a tough team. Their coach, Mike Ditka, always with a big wad of gum in his mouth, was the definition of tough. He even had a nickname to prove it: "Iron Mike." Ditka was a former tight end for the Bears, and he coached like he used to play: aggressive and in your face, with a temper that was always ready to blow.

Yet the coach and the architect of the Bears' defense was Buddy Ryan, the father of current Buffalo Bills head coach Rex Ryan and New Orleans Saints defensive coordinator Rob Ryan. Ryan was hot-tempered, intense, quick-witted, and funny. Most importantly, his players loved to play for him. He wanted them to attack, and attack they did.

There are twenty-two players on a football field, eleven on offense and eleven on defense. In 1985, two types of defensive formations ruled the league, the 3-4 (where three linemen were supported by four linebackers) and the 4-3 (where four linemen were supported by three linebackers). That left four defensive players in the secondary—two cornerbacks and two safeties.

Ryan, on the other hand, created something called

the "46" defense, named after Bears safety Doug Plank, who wore the number 46 on his jersey, and who at times would play the safety position close to the line of scrimmage, as though he were a linebacker. The 46 defense was based on a 4-3 setting, but it placed as many as eight players at the line. Since most offenses positioned six players at the line, the 46 allowed Chicago to attack with more players than the offense could block. The risk with playing eight players on the line was that it left only three players protecting the rest of the field, which left the Bears vulnerable if a receiver could get open quickly. Ryan's strategy was simple and ferocious: be quick enough and fast enough to overtake the offense before they had a chance to know what hit them. It wouldn't matter if a receiver got open quickly, because the quarterback wouldn't have the time to throw the ball to him.

And for one incredible season, that is exactly what happened.

In the season opener, the Bears trailed Tampa Bay 21–7 before storming back to win 38–28. In Week 2, they led the Patriots 20–0 before winning 20–7. They kept on cruising, winning week after week, including a 26–10 victory against the defending champion 49ers that put their record at 6-0 on the season.

Yet the Bears were just getting started. As the season progressed, their defense only seemed to grow stronger.

Up front were Richard Dent, a young defensive end who was powerful, quick, mean, and a future Hall of Famer; the tenacious defensive tackle Steve McMichael, who later became a pro wrestler, and McMichael's counterpart, William Perry, who was so big his nickname was "The Refrigerator." The Fridge loved to smile, he was funny, and the fans flocked to him. Weighing in at around 350 pounds (some said more), he was nearly impossible for any team to run the ball against.

In the secondary, there was the perennial Pro Bowl safety, Dave Duerson, who was just as good blitzing the quarterback as intercepting passes. Otis Wilson, a linebacker, was having the best season of his life, ripping the heads off running backs and anyone else who got in his way. The middle linebacker was the great Mike Singletary, another future Hall of Famer, who was the captain of the defense. He would go on to win Defensive Player of the Year twice in his career, earning his first in 1985.

The Bears were 9-0 after beating up on hated division rivals Green Bay and Minnesota, and people began talking about the possibility that the Bears would go undefeated. But more, people were talking about that defense, which attacked in waves, with speed and power and ferocity.

The Bears won again to make their record 10-0. Over their previous five games they had given up a total of 39 points, an average of under 8 points a game. How could you beat a team you could barely score against?

But the best was still to come.

On Sunday, November 17, the Bears went to Dallas to play the high-powered Cowboys on national television. What happened confirmed to everyone that the Cowboys no longer ranked in the top class of the NFC.

The Bears swarmed the Cowboys. The 46 defense rushed so many players at Dallas that the Cowboys players seemed scared even to have the ball in their hands, for fear of getting crunched by Wilson or Singletary or Wilber Marshall, another Chicago bruiser. The Bears' defense was like a train steamrolling through the Dallas offensive line. The entire country saw just how good the Bears really were. The final score: Chicago 44, Dallas 0.

The next week, the Bears beat Atlanta 36–0. Two consecutive shutouts in which the Bears had outscored the opposition by a combined total of 80 points.

The Bears were 12-0 and facing a Monday night showdown in Miami with the Dolphins, the team that had lost to San Francisco a year earlier in the Super Bowl. The high-scoring Dolphins were great, led by the young, rocket-armed quarterback Dan Marino.

The nation waited eagerly to see if anyone could even get a first down against these ferocious Bears.

The Dolphins managed that and quite a bit more, winning 38–24.

How could a team that outscored their last two opponents by 80 give up 38 points? The Miami game plan was brilliant. To offset the rush of Buddy Ryan's 46 defense, famed Miami coach Don Shula decided to make Marino roll out to his right to keep the Bears' defenders from overwhelming him. Moving Marino around gave him time to see the Chicago defense. Marino was famous for his ability to throw the ball very quickly.

By halftime, it was clear that Shula's strategy had thrown the Bears off their game. The score was 31–10.

The stunned Bears tried mounting a second-half comeback, but the deficit was too large to overcome. The Dolphins had pulled off the upset of the year.

There would be no undefeated season for Chicago.

Still, the Bears regrouped, won their final four games, and finished 15-1. When the playoffs started, they barely broke a sweat. In the first round, they hosted the New York Giants, another tough, defensive-minded team, and buried them, 21–0. Another shutout for the Bears' defense.

Next up: the NFC title game against the Los Angeles Rams. Another game, another shutout. The Bears won 24–0. They were 17-1, and heading to the Super Bowl for the first time ever.

When the Dolphins beat Chicago that Monday night in November, the entire football universe could only think of one thing: the Super Bowl. How great it would be, fans across America thought, if these two teams could have a rematch? The best offense against the best defense, with the added bonus of the Bears wanting revenge on the team that prevented them from going undefeated! It had to happen . . . right?

How was it possible, then, that Super Bowl XX found the Bears playing the New England Patriots?

The Patriots? *In the Super Bowl?*

This was long before the Patriots of Tom Brady and Bill Belichick. These Patriots had never been to the Super Bowl. That wasn't a big deal, because a lot of other teams hadn't, either. What *was* a big deal was that for the twenty seasons the Super Bowl had existed, the Patriots had never even reached the AFC Championship Game. They were anything but a winning franchise.

The Patriots didn't just lose, they lost badly and often. They had a losing record for nine of those twenty years. Between 1966 and 1985, the Patriots lost at least ten games seven times. They were founded in 1960—back then their name was the Boston Patriots—and in twenty-five years of existence had made the playoffs only four times.

But in 1985, the Patriots did something no Patriots team had ever done, something no Patriots fan had ever seen. They made a crazy run to the Super Bowl.

The Patriots had a young group of players: quarterback Tony Eason, running back Craig James, and wide receiver Irving Fryar. They were joined by veteran receiver Stanley Morgan, the great offensive lineman and future Hall of Famer John Hannah, and the veteran backup quarterback Steve Grogan. After splitting their first four games, they were beaten 24–20 by Cleveland to go 2-3. Yet they didn't let their losing record deter them. They proceeded to win their next six games, ultimately finishing the season 11-5, and clinching a playoff spot. They surprised teams that had traditionally been at the top, even beating Miami at home, 17–13, to improve their record to 6-3 at the time.

The Patriots beat the Jets 26–14 in the first round of the playoffs, then flew to Los Angeles to play the Raiders (the Raiders had moved to Los Angeles from Oakland in 1982), a team that had beaten them earlier in the season. Trailing 17–7 early, the Patriots battled back and stunned the Raiders 27–20 to reach the AFC championship for the first time ever.

But Miami awaited. And the game was in Miami.

The Patriots hadn't won a game in Miami in twenty years. To add to their underdog status, no team in NFL history had reached the Super Bowl by winning three road games. And, of course, the Dolphins had Marino.

But New England was determined to defy expectations. Patriots fans created a slogan for their impossible mission: "Squish the Fish." Amazingly, that's exactly what happened. The Patriots, playing with heart and fearlessness, crushed the Dolphins, 31–14.

So, the good news: the Patriots were heading to New Orleans to play in the Super Bowl for the first time in franchise history!

The bad news: They were playing the Chicago Bears, who were now 17-1. No one thought New England could win. They were huge underdogs, plain and simple. The Bears' defense was so good that they hadn't given up even a SINGLE POINT in the playoffs. Yet the Patriots were confident. Anything was possible if you believed in yourself and your team, right?

Wrong.

The Bears were too good. The Patriots scored first to take a 3–0 lead, and then they were hit with an avalanche. One Patriots turnover after another gave Chicago the field position they needed to capitalize. Forced fumbles turned into points on the scoreboard. It was 23–3 Bears at halftime. The Bears' defense was unforgiving, allowing just two pass completions, one first down, and 19 total yards.

Chicago never looked back. They were determined to win by a landslide.

They did. The Patriots kept on throwing interceptions and fumbling the ball, and the Bears kept on converting turnovers into touchdowns and field goals, displaying their greatness for all to see.

The Bears had been favored to win by 10 points. They won by 36.

The final score was 46–10, the worst loss by any team in Super Bowl history. The score was bad enough, but the images were worse. No team ever looked more overmatched than the Patriots. The Bears had knocked Eason out of the game entirely, and then devoured Grogan, sacking the two Patriots quarterbacks 7 times in total. The Patriots had 7 (7!) yards rushing for the entire game, and only 123 yards total. The Bears had 408. And to complete the embarrassment, the final points of the game were scored when Grogan was sacked in the end zone for a safety, 2 points that served as the cherry on top.

On their way off the playing field, the Bears players carried Ditka on their shoulders.

And they also carried Buddy Ryan.

It was fitting, because no other team had ever put

on such a season-long display of defensive excellence. It made sense that in the last game of the season, the biggest game of the year, the Bears played their best, most dominant football. Chicago was champion, and it was the first championship for any sports team in that city since 1963, when the Bears had won the NFL title.

After the Super Bowl, Ryan left to become coach of the Philadelphia Eagles. The Bears would be almost as good the following season with a 14-2 record, but they lost at home to Washington in their first playoff game. The Ditka Bears would never reach the Super Bowl again, would never be as good, as fearsome, or as dominant as they were in 1985.

But for one season, they were the most unstoppable team in the world.

SUPER BOWL XX
TOP TEN LIST

The Patriots had no chance against the Bears, and it was proof that a good defense could be just as dominant as a good offense, maybe more so. The Bears were stacked with Hall of Famers like linebacker Mike Singletary, defensive tackle Dan Hampton, and defensive end Richard Dent, who showed the world that defensive players could make or break a championship team. Here is a list of defensive players who changed the course of professional football history.

1. Deion Sanders (cornerback, 1989–2005): In a passing league, he revolutionized the cornerback position by establishing himself as an invaluable player who could shut down receivers.

2. Reggie White (defensive end, 1985–2000): Second all-time in sacks, but the most dominant defensive lineman ever. Helped lead the Green

Bay defense to two Super Bowl appearances and one victory.

3. Mike Singletary (linebacker, 1981–1992): Formidable captain of the Bears' defense. He was a tenacious tackling machine.

4. Ronnie Lott (safety, 1981–1994): One of the hardest-hitting safeties in league history. Four-time Super Bowl winner with the 49ers.

5. Mean Joe Greene (defensive end, 1969–1981): Signature pass rusher of the famed Pittsburgh Steel Curtain defense. He was a dangerous force on the field who was feared by opposing defenses due to his huge build and intense style of play.

6. Ray Lewis (linebacker, 1996–2012): Emotional leader of the Ravens' defense. Two-time Super Bowl champion. He could do it all: record tackles, sacks, force fumbles, and make interceptions.

7. Rod Woodson (cornerback/safety, 1987–2003): Smart, attacking defensive back known for making interceptions.

8. Lawrence Taylor (linebacker, 1981–1993): Revolutionized the linebacker position with his speed, athleticism, and ability to sack the QB.

9. Bruce Smith (defensive end, 1985–2003): Pro-

Bowl leader and dominant pass rusher on classic
Bills teams of the 1990s. All-time sacks leader.

10. J. J. Watt (defensive end, 2011–present): Rising
superstar on his way to becoming an all-time
great. Won the NFL Defensive Player of the Year
Award twice in only four seasons.

SUPER BOWL XXII
THE PIONEER

~~~~~~~~~~~~~~~~~~~~~~~~~~~~~~~~

WASHINGTON VS.
DENVER BRONCOS

The best part about sports is the fantasy it creates in our minds. Like the excitement of playing in the backyard, dreaming about being famous one day, of catching the winning pass, hitting the game-ending home run, or sinking the buzzer-beating basket. It's the joy of letting your imagination go wild, picturing being lifted up in the air by your teammates, hoisting the championship trophy as the crowd chants your name.

But sometimes, sports are more about reality than fantasy. Sometimes, the fun and games of sports are interrupted by serious issues that must be confronted.

Even though people in the game always said sports were ahead of society because teams wanted to win and would always play the best player, no matter his race, that boast turned out to be more wishful thinking than actual truth. For many years, in fact, it was often skin color that determined which players were chosen to fill certain positions in the NFL. Speed positions were usually African American.

And quarterbacks were white.

Why? Because inside the NFL lived a longstanding attitude that African Americans were not as smart as white players. Many coaches believed an African American would be unable to process the information a quarterback needs to succeed as quickly and as well as a white quarterback. Furthermore, executives did not believe that white players would respond and follow the lead of African Americans. Thus, no head coaches who were black. And certainly no quarterbacks.

These reasons and more explain why Super Bowl XXII was more than just a football game. The Washington quarterback, Doug Williams, was the first African American quarterback to start a Super Bowl game.

Williams was no stranger to success. He had started his career with the Tampa Bay Buccaneers, a team that was founded in 1976 and lost all of its games that first season. Williams, a graduate of Grambling State University, a traditionally all-black college in Louisiana, took over as quarterback two years later, and under his leadership the Bucs not only made the playoffs for the first time in their history, they actually went to the NFC Championship Game in 1979, losing to the Super Bowl-bound Rams.

But Williams and the city of Tampa Bay did not get along. As an African American quarterback, Williams felt his mistakes were less acceptable to the team and its fans. Even though he had helped make the Bucs a successful team, the relationship was not a warm one. After heated contract negotiations, in which the Bucs offered Williams a salary that would have kept him among the lowest-paid starters in the league, the two sides parted ways.

The pressure mounted and Williams left football, only to return one year later, but not to the NFL. Instead, Williams signed with the rival US Football League (USFL). He played two seasons for the Oklahoma/Arizona Outlaws, but after the USFL went out of business in 1985, Williams returned to the NFL, signing with Washington because he had a good relationship with the coach, Joe Gibbs.

It had been only three years since Washington had reached back-to-back Super Bowls, beating Miami in Super Bowl XVII before getting blown out by the Raiders in Super Bowl XVIII. They had come close to making the Big Game again just the season before— reaching the NFC Championship Game, only to lose to the eventual Super Bowl champion New York Giants. So the memories of high achievements and expectations were still fresh in their minds.

They had a talented group of players determined to keep the good times rolling. On defense, Washington had the Hall of Fame cornerback Darrell Green, one of the fastest players in the league, and defensive ends Charles Mann and Dexter Manley, masters of the art of sacking. The wide receivers Ricky Sanders, Art Monk, and Gary Clark were explosive and sure-handed. The offensive line, averaging nearly 320 pounds per player, was given the perfect nickname by the fans: "The Hogs."

But the NFC, especially the NFC East division, was

a tough place to win. The Cowboys were no longer a playoff-caliber team, but Philadelphia was strong, and of course the Giants were the defending Super Bowl champs. Washington was talented, too, but troubled. At the start of the season, the team didn't even use Williams. He was the backup to Jay Schroeder, Washington's young starting quarterback. Then Schroeder hurt his shoulder in the opening game of the season, against Philadelphia—and what followed was a fracture that affected the entire team. Schroeder was looked at as the team's star on the rise. Yet the veterans on the team preferred the steady Williams as their quarterback. And the competition between the two quarterbacks was anything but friendly, stemming back to the previous season's NFC Championship Game, when Schroeder, seemingly injured, lashed out at Williams after coaches had sent him into the game to replace the young quarterback.

The division between Schroeder and Williams was not the only one brewing in the NFL at the time. As a whole, the players in the league did not believe they were being treated fairly. The disagreement was rooted in contract negotiations. When their contracts were up, players wanted the freedom to go to another team, to be free agents, just like everyday people have the right to change jobs. The team owners said no.

The owners were unwilling to negotiate, yet they expected their teams to keep on playing. But the players weren't having it. So, during the season, before the third game, the players refused to come to work; they went on strike. NFL teams responded by finding substitutes—guys who were not as good as the regular NFL players, but were willing to take the jobs of players who were fighting for better working conditions. They were called "replacement players," and the games they played counted in the standings.

The strike lasted just three games. Many players, unwilling to support each other, began returning in the second week of the strike. Some had not joined in at all.

On the field, Washington was 3-0 with replacement players, and when the regular NFL players returned, the question of who should be the starting quarterback, Williams or Schroeder, resurfaced.

Gibbs couldn't make up his mind. Then Williams suffered a back injury. He felt he could still play, yet Gibbs chose to go with Schroeder the rest of the way.

Williams had played well, but had lost his only two starts of the season. Schroeder, meanwhile, seemed to have a winning touch.

Schroeder was inconsistent, though, and after a troubling performance and a loss against the Dolphins in the second to last game of the season, Gibbs went back to Williams for the season finale. Washington won against a very good Minnesota Vikings team, and Williams was named the starter for the playoffs.

They went to Chicago and won a hard-fought game, 21–17. Then, in an NFC championship match dominated by defense, Washington squeaked by Minnesota 17–10 to reach the Super Bowl. Awaiting them were John Elway and the Denver Broncos.

The Broncos were sore from their Super Bowl loss to the Giants the year before. 1986 had been an amazing year that ended in supreme disappointment. In the AFC championship against Cleveland, John Elway, their young quarterback, became a legend by driving his team nearly the entire length of the field—98 yards—in the final minutes to save the season. Elway was so good and so clutch that his last-minute comeback would forever be known simply as "The Drive."

But in the Super Bowl, against the Giants, the

Broncos got flattened, 39–20. The entire 1987 season would be dedicated to getting back to the Super Bowl, and this time, winning it.

They went 10-4-1, winning the AFC West division. The core of the team was back. The defense was dominated by three players: Pro Bowl linebacker Karl Mecklenburg, defensive end Rulon Jones, and hard-hitting safety Dennis Smith. The offense was led by Elway, who relied on a trio of receivers nicknamed "The Three Amigos": Vance Johnson, Ricky Nattiel, and Mark Jackson.

These Broncos were sensational. They played like a team hungry to get back to the Super Bowl, hungry to win after losing in such a frustrating way. They opened the playoffs by destroying Houston, 34–10, in a game that wasn't even as close as the lopsided score.

That set up an AFC Championship Game rematch with Cleveland, the same Cleveland team Elway had beaten a year before with The Drive. The Browns were seeking revenge for that heartbreaking loss and hoping to play in their first Super Bowl. The game was another close one, but the Broncos won again, this time 38–33, and secured their return ticket to the Super Bowl. With such a talented team, led by one of the greatest quarterbacks ever to play, Denver was heavily favored to win over Washington, a team that didn't seem to know which quarterback it wanted to use.

The Broncos hit the ground running and started out on fire. On the first play of their first possession, Elway dropped back and threw a 56-yard touchdown pass to Nattiel. On their second possession, they kicked a field goal. Two possessions, two scores, and just like that Denver led, 10–0. The Denver defense plugged up Washington's offensive attack once more. The Broncos got the ball back and nearly scored again, but Elway was sacked, forcing a punt.

Throughout Super Bowl week, the writers and TV cameras focused on Williams, the first African American quarterback to start in a Super Bowl.

But maybe the pressure was getting to him—the game was going miserably. Not only was Washington trailing 10–0 in the first quarter, but also, Williams took a hard sack, hurt his knee, and had to leave the game. His team was losing. He was hurt. The battle to be the leader of the team seemed to be falling apart in the biggest game of the year. Williams's chance to make history was rapidly slipping away.

Then came the second quarter, and with it, out

of nowhere, came the greatest performance in Super Bowl history.

On the team's first possession, Williams dropped back and threw a deep pass to Ricky Sanders for an 80-yard touchdown. Washington had its first points. It took just a single play to change the feeling in the air.

On their second possession, Williams hit Clark for a 27-yard touchdown, and Washington had its first lead of the game, 14–10.

On their third possession, Timmy Smith, a reserve running back who had played in only seven games all season, starting none of them, broke off a 58-yard run for a touchdown, and Washington's lead was 21–10.

The Broncos didn't know what hit them.

What hit them was Williams—he had Denver's number.

On their next possession, Williams launched another bomb and hit Sanders again, this time for 50 yards.

28–10.

Then Elway threw an interception. After coming out of the gate in such an impressive manner, the tides had turned. It seemed as though nothing could go right for the Broncos.

The opposite was true for Williams and Washington. It was almost like they could do no wrong. Williams got the ball again, and threw yet another touchdown pass, this one to tight end Clint Didier.

Five possessions, 5 touchdowns. Down 10–0 at the end of the first quarter, Washington went to halftime up 35–10. The game, for all intents and purposes, was over.

The team broke record after record. Elway and the Broncos were crushed, humiliated, and never recovered from the second-quarter onslaught. The final score was 42–10.

Smith rushed for 204 yards, a Super Bowl record. And yet it was Williams, who threw for 340 yards and 4 touchdowns, who was named Super Bowl MVP.

It was a personal and national triumph for Williams. On a personal level, he had started the year unsure whether anyone even wanted him on the team, but at the end of it, by continuing to believe in himself and his ability to be a good player, he emerged as the best player on the best team.

On a national level, Williams proved that all the critics were wrong. All of the people in football who'd believed for years that a black person could not be a good quarterback were shown how false their claims were. Williams put on one of the greatest performances in Super Bowl history, and became the first African American quarterback to win the Big Game.

SUPER BOWL XXII
TOP TEN LIST

Doug Williams changed football history by being the first African American quarterback to win the Super Bowl, but he wasn't the only person to have a profound effect on the history and direction of how football is played and viewed today. Here is a list of ten other pioneers who made us look at the NFL differently.

1. Bill Walsh: Architect of the 49ers dynasty and the West Coast offense.
2. Tony Dungy: The first African American head coach to win a Super Bowl.
3. Jimmy Johnson: Dallas coach who revolutionized speed on defense in the early 1990s.
4. Bo Jackson: The phenom who played two professional sports: football and baseball.
5. Tony Gonzalez: Changed the tight end position

into one that emphasized speed in addition to strength.

6. Deion Sanders: Baseball player, kick returner, greatest cover cornerback in history.

7. Lawrence Taylor: Revolutionized the linebacker position with the New York Giants.

8. Roger Craig: Redefined the running back position by becoming the first player ever to record 1,000 rushing yards and 1,000 receiving yards in the same season.

9. Fran Tarkenton: Prolific passer and scrambling quarterback for the Minnesota Vikings.

10. Tom Landry: Architect of the Dallas Cowboys dynasty who revived the shotgun formation seen today in almost every NFL game.

SUPER BOWL XXIV PERFECTION

~~~~~~

SAN FRANCISCO 49ERS VS. DENVER BRONCOS

What was so interesting about the 1989 season was that the 49ers were in the middle of a transition. The year before, San Francisco had won its third Super Bowl, beating Cincinnati 20–16 in a thriller. The 49ers had been trailing 16–13 in the final minutes, deep in their own territory. The Bengals watched anxiously as the clock ticked down, mere minutes away from their first-ever Super Bowl title.

When the 49ers got the ball back, with the length of the field to travel, Montana was in great spirits, confident that San Francisco would move the ball, confident that he would lead his team to victory. His teammates were amazed that Montana didn't even appear nervous.

That's how Joe Montana earned the nickname "Joe Cool."

Montana marched San Francisco down the field, hitting John Taylor with a 10-yard touchdown pass to complete the comeback and become champions once more.

The transition came after the game, when Walsh said he would not be returning the following year to coach the defending champions. Instead, the defensive coordinator, George Seifert, who had never been a head coach before, would take over the team. The 49ers and their fans wondered how the team would fare after such an important loss.

It turned out they had no reason to worry. Even without the great Walsh, San Francisco didn't falter. Led by Montana, who only seemed to be getting better, the 49ers finished the regular season 14-2. Montana finished the season with the highest single-season quarterback rating ever (a mark that has since been bettered multiple times) and was named the NFL's MVP. He had weapons galore, including running back Roger Craig, tight end Brent Jones, wide receiver John Taylor, and perhaps the greatest wide receiver in history, Jerry Rice. Not surprisingly, the team had the league's number-one ranked offense in '89.

Rice, who had played college ball for tiny Mississippi Valley State, was the 49ers' top pick in the 1985 draft . His father was a brickmason, and the family lived in Crawford, one of the more remote areas of the Deep South. Rice always said his great hands came from working in his father's business, tossing bricks to him.

Montana was the star, driven to win, but no one, perhaps not even Walsh, understood how bad Jerry Rice wanted to be great. Rice's early struggles catching the football stemmed, Walsh always said, from wanting to be great *too* much. He couldn't relax. He couldn't concentrate. He was a perfectionist who was incredibly hard on himself whenever he made a mistake, making it difficult to concentrate on the next play.

Rice struggled early. His speed times were slower than expected, and some football executives thought maybe he wasn't going to be as good as the forecasts.

When the season started, Rice didn't catch his first touchdown pass until Week 5. He didn't catch more than 4 passes in a game until a December breakout against the Rams, in which he caught 10 passes for 241 in a 27–20 loss. In two of his final games, though, Rice tallied more than 100 yards receiving. He was on the brink of success.

When Rice put it together in 1986, it was clear just how good he could be. Rice totaled six 100-yard receiving games, one 200-yard receiving game, and another for 150. With his great hands and knack for racking up yards, it became apparent Rice was the missing piece San Francisco's offense had needed.

The 49ers' offense was outstanding, but the defense was no slouch, either. Led by All-Pros Ronnie Lott at safety, Don Griffin at cornerback, and Michael Walter at linebacker, the team had the league's number-three ranked defense. It was a team seemingly without weakness.

With all of the pieces in place, the 1989 season was magical. In the first game of the season, the 49ers were in Indianapolis playing the Colts. The 49ers led 23–10 when Indy cut the lead to 23–17. Then the Colts' defense came alive and pushed the 49ers back, and on third down, with the crowd screaming like maniacs, Montana dropped back and hit Rice on a short crossing route over the middle. Rice caught the ball in stride and ran 58 yards for a game-breaking touchdown. The 49ers won, 30–24.

Two weeks later, the 49ers went into Philadelphia, a rough, tough place to play, and took on the Eagles, who were now coached by Buddy Ryan, the old defensive coordinator of the '85 Bears.

The Philadelphia defense was impressive, led by defensive end Reggie White, an ordained minister who earned the nickname "Minister of Defense." White was one of the greatest defensive players in the history of the game, and finished second all-time in total sacks. White was joined by defensive tackle Jerome Brown and safeties Wes Hopkins and Todd Bell. The Eagles played the same "46" defense as Ryan's Bears teams. Their defense was stacked with very good athletes who were strong enough and fast enough to pressure the quarterback the way Chicago once had.

The Eagles mauled the 49ers during the first three quarters of the game. By the end of the third quarter, Philadelphia had sacked Montana *eight* times.

According to Harris Barton, one of San Francisco's offensive linemen, Montana had "that glazed-over" look that comes with getting hit too hard. The Eagles led 21–10 entering the fourth quarter.

Then Montana, bruised and bloody, went to work.

He hit John Taylor with a 70-yard bomb for a touchdown. The Eagles responded to make it 28–17.

Joe Cool was unfazed. He came right back out and threw another touchdown, this time to Tom Rathman.

Then he threw another, a 25-yarder to Brent Jones, and finally, a 33-yarder to Rice. It was a brilliant comeback.

The final score was San Francisco 38, Philadelphia 28. Montana had been beaten up so badly that the 49ers thought he would never make it through the game, but he showed just how tough he really was by throwing four touchdowns in the fourth quarter alone. He finished with 428 passing yards and five touchdowns for the game.

The Niners rolled through the rest of the season, scoring 30 points eight times. They were 8-0 on the road and prided themselves on being that rare California team that could play in the snow and cold of the East Coast and Midwest.

One night, their hated rivals, the Los Angeles Rams, who had already beaten them once during the season, led 27–10 in the fourth quarter. Again, the 49ers were being beaten up on the road.

And again, Montana mounted a defiant comeback. Having already completed a 93-yard touchdown pass to Taylor in the second quarter, Montana hit Mike Wilson for a 7-yard touchdown to make it 27–17. Then, standing near his own goal line, he did it again, finding Taylor for a short gain, and in 49er style, Taylor broke free and ran for a 95-yard touchdown, cutting the Rams' lead to 27–23. Finishing off the comeback, Montana drove the 49ers downfield once more, and scored again to seal the 30–27 win.

Yes, the 49ers were terrific through the regular season, but the playoffs were when they really kicked it into high gear. In the first round, San Francisco demolished the Vikings, 41–13, to set up a rematch with the Rams for the third time that season, the teams having split the previous two. This grudge match for all the marbles was filled with tension. You could feel it in the air as the Rams took an early 3–0 lead.

Maybe Los Angeles could pull off the upset?

Nah. No chance.

The 49ers showed no mercy. They scored the next 30 points in a row and didn't give up another score to the Rams for the rest of the game. In the 30–3 win, Montana threw 31 passes, completing 27 of them. San Francisco was going back to the Super Bowl.

The Denver Broncos, on the other hand, were a good but shaken team. Each year, they had been at or near the top of the AFC, only to be humiliated in the Super Bowl. Like San Francisco, the Broncos had a spectacular quarterback in John Elway. Unlike San Francisco, the Broncos never showed up in the Big Game. In 1986, they advanced to the Super Bowl, only to lose to the Giants 39–20. The next year, they made it all the way back to the Super Bowl, hoping for redemption, but all they ended up with was a blowout loss at the hands of Washington, 42–10.

In 1989, the Broncos went 11-5 in the regular season and narrowly escaped Pittsburgh 24–23 in the divisional round. In the AFC championship, facing rival Cleveland, the team whose heart Denver had broken twice before, Denver prepared for another battle. But contrary to expectations, the Broncos won easily, 37–21.

That put them in the Super Bowl for the third time in four years. Heading into the game, they were considerable underdogs—the 49ers were favored by 13 points.

Could the Broncos defy the odds?

Unfortunately for Denver, they ended up sharing the same fate as the Los Angeles Rams.

San Francisco did not disappoint. They scored at least 13 points in every quarter. Rice scored three touchdowns, and Taylor, Roger Craig, and Tom Rathman each scored one.

The defense produced four turnovers. Montana went 24 for 32 with 317 passing yards and five touchdowns. The score was 27–3 at halftime, and 55–10 at the final gun.

Elway, for all of his greatness, was helpless. There was no stopping these 49ers. The Broncos had no chance.

When the Chicago Bears destroyed the Patriots in Super Bowl XX at the Louisiana Superdome, most people thought that Chicago had played the perfect game of football, one so amazing and dominant that it would be a long, long time before anyone witnessed such a moment again.

No one thought such perfection could be matched in less than five years.

And yet when the Super Bowl returned to New Orleans in 1990, when the San Francisco 49ers won their fourth Super Bowl in four tries, it turned out the Super Bowl XX Bears weren't complete perfection after all.

The 49ers had outdone them.

The Bears were a dominating team, led by their dominating defense. The 49ers, however, appeared to master the game both offensively and defensively on their way to becoming the signature team of the 1980s.

And it was all on display on that day in 1990. The game was never in doubt. The 49ers destroyed the Broncos 55–10, the largest margin of victory in Super Bowl history, topping the 36-point difference between the Bears and the Patriots in Super Bowl XX. In winning, the 49ers joined the Steelers as the only teams in NFL history to win four Super Bowls, becoming the first team to win back-to-back championships since the Steelers did it in 1978 and 1979. The win solidified Joe Montana as the greatest postseason quarterback in history and, some might argue, quite possibly the best quarterback of all time.

San Francisco had not only won their fourth Super

Bowl, but had done so in such a complete fashion that they had assured themselves the status of legends. Walsh was gone, but his system lived on. Rice and Montana had sealed their legacies as two of the greatest players to ever step on a football field. Seifert was transformed from dutiful assistant to Super Bowl–winning coach. Lott was a clear-cut Hall of Famer.

The victory marked the completion of the 49ers' great transformation over the previous thirteen years. A team that had once been considered losers emerged as one of the greatest, most innovative dynasties in the history of sports. The 49ers' West Coast offense, created by Bill Walsh, was emulated by teams across the league. Other teams, like Washington, had won Super Bowls in the 1980s, but San Francisco had been in the hunt virtually every season, winning at least ten games every year throughout the decade. In short, Super Bowl XXIV was the celebration of that dominance.

The dynasty would continue, but with a different cast and different competition, most notably the Dallas Cowboys, a team that rediscovered its greatness. Steve Young, Montana's backup, was increasingly seen as the successor. Montana would never reach the Super Bowl again, overcome by age, injury, and a painful loss the next year to the New York Giants that ended the 49ers' chance to become the first team ever to win three straight Super Bowls. Montana was traded to Kansas City after the 1992 season. He would play two more years and simply retire with four Super Bowl championships, no defeats, and a reputation as the best quarterback to ever play the game.

SUPER BOWL XXIV
TOP TEN LIST

San Francisco destroyed Denver to win the Super Bowl, and in the process showed the world what a dominant offense could do on its best day. Here are some other offenses that gave defenses fits and made history.

1. 1999 St. Louis Rams: Scored 32.9 points per game, beat teams by an average of 17.8. Won the Super Bowl.
2. 2007 New England Patriots: Scored a record 589 total points, 36.8 points per game. Tom Brady threw for 50 touchdown passes, 23 of them to Randy Moss.
3. 1983 Washington: Scored 541 total points. John Riggins rushed for 24 touchdowns.
4. 2001 St. Louis Rams: Scored 503 total points. Kurt Warner threw for 36 touchdowns. Marshall Faulk ran for 1,382 yards.

5. 1984 San Francisco 49ers: Went 15-1. Joe Montana was named Super Bowl MVP. Roger Craig became a star.

6. 1981 San Diego Chargers: Averaged 29.9 points per game. Wide receiver Charlie Joiner and tight end Kellen Winslow recorded over 1,000 yards receiving, and running back Chuck Muncie ran for more than 1,000 yards.

7. 1984 Miami Dolphins: Dan Marino threw 48 touchdowns and led his team to the Super Bowl.

8. 2009 New Orleans Saints: Scored 513 total points. Drew Brees threw for 34 touchdowns. Four players recorded 500 receiving yards. Won the Super Bowl.

9. 1998 Minnesota Vikings: The combination of Randall Cunningham to Randy Moss and Cris Carter led the team to 556 total points, an average of 34.8 per game.

10. 1998 Denver Broncos: 501 total points. One of the greatest quarterback–running back–tight end combinations in league history with John Elway, Terrell Davis, and Shannon Sharpe. Won the Super Bowl.

THIRD DOWN

SUPER BOWL XXVII
THE RETURN OF
THE STAR

~~~~~~~~~~~~~~~~~~~~~~~~~~~~~~~~~~~~~

DALLAS COWBOYS VS.
BUFFALO BILLS

Following that fateful Sunday in 1985 when the Chicago Bears destroyed the Cowboys in Week 11, 44–0, some people thought Dallas's days of greatness were finished for good. But despite the Cowboys suffering their worst loss in franchise history and first shutout in fifteen years, they had accomplished too much and had too much pride as an organization to stay down for long. From 1966, when the Cowboys made the playoffs for the first time as a franchise, until 1985, they earned a spot in the playoffs eighteen times, reached the NFC title game twelve times, advanced to the Super Bowl six times, and won twice.

No wonder they became known as America's Team.

However, so many of the names that made the Cowboys famous leading up to 1985 were gone, and the ones that remained were older and declining. Roger Staubach was long retired. Tony Dorsett, their all-time leading rusher, was nearing the end of his career. The pillars of the "Doomsday Defense," including nine-time Pro Bowl defensive tackle Randy White, his formidable counterpart at defensive tackle, Big John Dutton, and the defensive end Ed "Too Tall" Jones were all in their thirties and playing out the twilight of their careers.

Still, Dallas managed to win the NFC East division that next season, only to lose 20–0 to the Los Angeles Rams, the first time a Dallas team had ever been shut out in a playoff game. Things were falling apart for the most famous name in football.

The next year, in 1986, not only did the Cowboys fail to make the playoffs, but they finished 7-9, their first losing record since 1964. That same year, the Cowboys acquired the great running back Herschel Walker when the United States Football League folded.

Yet the addition of Walker wasn't nearly enough to overcome the loss of so many talented players.

For the next four years, the great and proud Dallas Cowboys would lose and lose and lose. In 1988, the Cowboys hit rock bottom, going 3-13.

Tom Landry, the only coach the Cowboys had ever had, was fired. Landry had been the very heart of the Dallas Cowboys. He was part of the old days of football, of coaches wearing sport-jackets and ties on the sideline, days that had passed him and the organization by.

It was time to say good-bye to the old Dallas traditions. If the Cowboys were going to be good again, they had to rebuild everything from the ground up. So Dallas began the new era by hiring Jimmy Johnson, a brilliant football mind who coached the University of Miami.

The Cowboys were just getting started turning over a new leaf. Four games into the 1989 season, the Cowboys traded the most valuable player they had, Walker, to Minnesota in the biggest trade in the history of the NFL: eighteen players and six—yes, six—future draft picks. Minnesota felt they had received the better end of the deal. The Vikings were a good team before the trade, but they hoped that by adding a player like Walker they'd found the missing piece they needed to go all the way.

It didn't happen. The Vikings would never reach the Super Bowl with Walker.

On the other hand, the picks Dallas received from Minnesota rebuilt the franchise and eventually put the Cowboys back on top.

It didn't happen immediately. In 1989, Johnson's first season as head coach, Dallas won just one game and lost fifteen, but Johnson had faith. He had a quarterback from UCLA, Troy Aikman, who showed promise. He was reunited with a wide receiver he'd coached at the University of Miami, Michael Irvin, who was a big target and had the chance to be an excellent player. The team was stacked with young, promising talent on both sides of the ball, including center Mark Stepnoski and linebacker Ken Norton Jr., whose father was a boxer who'd once beat Muhammad Ali!

But how could anyone be excited about a team that won one lousy game? Easily.

The next year, Dallas won seven games, bolstered by Emmitt Smith, a young running back from the University of Florida acquired with one of the draft choices from the Walker trade. In addition to his excellent running skills, Smith was also a solid receiver and an effective blocker.

Dallas continued to improve from one year to the next. In 1991, they won eleven games, adding another player from the Walker trade, wide receiver Alvin Harper. Along with Irvin, Aikman now had two big targets in the passing game. Dallas also acquired talented tight end Jay Novacek from the Cardinals. The team was coming together.

Vastly improved though they were, Dallas still hadn't fully reemerged as a great team. So it was no surprise to anyone, except perhaps to the confident Cowboys, that Dallas lost to Detroit in the 1991 playoffs.

In 1992, though, many of the young guys they'd acquired over the previous three years blossomed into outstanding players. That year, the Cowboys stormed the NFL, winning thirteen games.

In his third season, Smith became a star, rushing for 1,713 yards and 18 touchdowns. He wasn't very fast, but he made up for his lack of speed in other ways. When he had the ball in his hands he found ways to escape and run by defenders. Aikman also began to shine, throwing for 23 touchdowns. Irvin caught 78 passes for 1396 yards and proved that his coach had made a wise decision in recruiting the receiver in their college days.

More than that, Johnson had an idea to change the way defense was played in football. In the past, defense was about power first, speed second. Johnson decided to draft big players who could not only hit, but also run sideline to sideline as fast as any running back. Norton was the best example. With this new breed of defenders, the Cowboys surprised teams with their ability to cover fast receivers, and keep them from getting around corners, which often prevented long gains. It took six sometimes painful years, but the Cowboys looked like they were finally back.

They took revenge on teams that had humiliated them when they were down, chief among them Philadelphia. Dallas took great pleasure in crushing the Eagles 34–10 in the divisional playoffs, setting up an NFC Championship showdown with the great dynasty, the San Francisco 49ers, in San Francisco.

The Cowboys and 49ers hadn't met in the playoffs since the 1981 season, when Joe Montana hit Dwight Clark with "The Catch," which broke Dallas's heart and started the 49ers' dynasty. Now, Montana, injured most of the year, had lost his job to Steve Young, the backup quarterback who was the future of the 49ers. For the biggest game of the year, Joe Montana, arguably the greatest quarterback who ever lived, the man who owned all four 49ers Super Bowl rings, stood on the sidelines.

On the other sideline, as the honorary captain for Dallas, was the legend Roger Staubach.

To become a dynasty, you have to take down the reigning dynasty. On that afternoon, the 49ers found out just how good and talented this young Cowboys team was. In the rain and mud at Candlestick Park, the Cowboys fought. The 49ers led early, but the Cowboys came back. Their speed and quickness on defense, combined with the wet weather, led to costly fumbles and interceptions for the 49ers.

Dallas scored a field goal early, but San Francisco capitalized on a 50-yard kickoff return, driving 48 yards for a touchdown. The 49ers led, 7–3. Then Dallas came right back, taking advantage of a 49ers turnover. Emmitt Smith danced into the end zone and the Cowboys jumped ahead, 10–7. The teams were tied at halftime, 10–10.

After a first-half stalemate, Dallas took over in the second half. Smith ran through the 49ers, showing off his excellent vision and ability to pick up second-effort yards on plays that appeared to be going nowhere. The Cowboys led 24–13 in the fourth.

Even so, the game wasn't out of reach quite yet. The 49ers' championship mentality wouldn't let them quit, and with seven minutes left, they made a charge. Young hit Rice to keep the drive going, and the completions kept on coming. One to tight end Brent Jones, a pair to running back Ricky Watters, and to cap off the drive, Young hit Rice again to make the score 24–20 with 4:22 left. Could the 49ers break the Cowboys' hearts again, like Montana had eleven years earlier?

Jimmy Johnson wasn't interested in giving San Francisco a chance. On Dallas's first play, Johnson went for the win. Instead of running the ball and killing time off the clock, a decision that could potentially have given the 49ers a chance to get the ball back, Aikman dropped back to pass and hit Alvin Harper on a slant route. The 49ers were unprepared for such a bold decision. Cornerback Don Griffin slipped and fell in the mud. Dana Hall, the safety who was supposed to protect the middle of the field, was late reacting and Harper sped away for 70 yards. That play finished the 49ers. The final score was 30–20.

Three years earlier, the Cowboys had gone 1-15. Now, they were going to the Super Bowl. The Star was back.

They would play the hungry, desperate Buffalo Bills, a team that suffered a gut-wrenching Super Bowl loss two years before against the New York Giants. In the final seconds of that game, Buffalo's kicker, Scott Norwood, missed what would've been a game-winning 47-yard field goal. They lost 20–19. The next year, the Bills went back to the Super Bowl, only to be beaten handily by Washington, 37–24.

So the Bills had gone to consecutive Super Bowls and lost both. Denver had done the same in '86 and '87, but no team in history had ever lost three straight Super Bowls.

It's hard enough to return to the Super Bowl— only a handful of teams have ever done it. It's even harder still to return to the Super Bowl after losing not once, but twice in a row. But Buffalo did. They put the pain of losing two Super Bowls behind them and went to work on winning in their third attempt.

It was no coincidence that Buffalo was heading to its third consecutive Super Bowl. The Bills were one loaded football team. Like Dallas with Troy Aikman,

Buffalo had a quarterback that would go to the Hall of Fame, Jim "Machine Gun" Kelly. Like Dallas with Emmitt Smith, they had a running back who would go to the Hall of Fame, Thurman Thomas. The list went on and on, both teams featuring future Hall of Fame players on offense and defense. Dallas had Charles Haley. Buffalo had dominating defensive end Bruce Smith. To match Michael Irvin, the Bills had Andre Reed, a receiver who finished his career eleventh all-time in touchdown receptions. And like Dallas, the Bills had fast, well-known linebackers in Cornelius Bennett and Darryl Talley. They had it all.

Even their coach, Marv Levy, wound up in the Hall of Fame.

With so much talent, it was no surprise that the Bills went 13-3 in 1990 and again in 1991. Yet by 1992, Buffalo had slipped a little bit, and failed to win their division. They still managed to go 11-5 and make the playoffs, but their year ended on a low note. In the last game of the regular season, Kelly was injured in a 27–3 loss to Houston.

And when the playoffs started, they played Houston again. Frank Reich, the backup quarterback, started for Kelly. A great talent sat on the sidelines, and morale was weak, so it was no surprise that the Bills were beaten down early by the Oilers. In the third quarter, with Buffalo already down 28–3, Houston safety Bubba McDowell intercepted Reich to extend their lead to 35–3.

Down a colossal THIRTY-TWO points, the season looked over for the Bills.

Or was it?

Suddenly, Reich erupted and the Oilers collapsed both offensively and defensively. The Bills used every ounce of talent they possessed and all the tools at their disposal to try to mount a comeback. The tide started to turn when Buffalo's backup running back, Kenneth Davis, narrowly ran past the left pylon and into the end zone to score a touchdown.

Still down 25 points, the Bills had a ways to go if they were to have any hope of staying alive. So on the kickoff after the score, Buffalo took a gamble . . . and it paid off. The Bills kicker, Steve Christie, let loose an onsides kick that was recovered by Christie himself! Four plays later, Reich launched a bomb to wide receiver Don Beebe, connecting for a 38-yard touchdown.

The Bills scored unanswered touchdown after unanswered touchdown. In less than a quarter, Buffalo cut Houston's lead by *twenty-eight* points!

Then, with three minutes left to play, Reich hit Reed for his second touchdown catch of the game. After falling behind by 32 points, the Bills, like an unstoppable force, came back to gain the lead, 38–35!

But somehow, with time and morale running out, Houston gathered themselves and put together a 63-yard drive that ended with a game-tying field goal as the game clock ticked down.

Overtime.

Houston started with the ball, but squandered their chance, throwing an interception in their own territory. A few minutes later, the Bills sealed the deal and the comeback, hitting an easy field goal to win.

The Bills had come all the way back, winning 41–38 in overtime. The stadium exploded with shouts and cheers.

After taking a 35–3 lead, Houston had scored just three points the rest of the game.

To this day, it is still the greatest playoff comeback in the history of the NFL.

Maybe this was Buffalo's year! If a team could

come back from being down 35–3, maybe no one could beat them.

Neither Pittsburgh nor Miami could manage to overcome the Bills in the playoffs, and Buffalo earned their third straight trip to the Super Bowl.

On the biggest stage in all of sports, the Bills and Cowboys were both motivated. The Bills wanted to make that third time the lucky one, and the Cowboys hadn't been back to the Super Bowl since 1979.

Unfortunately for Buffalo, the third time wasn't the charm. Despite the momentum that had pushed them into the Super Bowl, they ran into a brick wall in the form of the mighty Cowboys. The game was a blowout. Dallas was fast. Buffalo was sloppy. The Cowboys, led by Johnson, played with no fear. The same could not be said of Kelly who, back from injury, threw four interceptions. Combined with the team's five lost fumbles, the Bills coughed up the ball for a total of nine turnovers!

Nothing good ever comes out of nine turnovers.

The final score was a whopping 52–17. The Cowboys had scored the most points in a single game in Super Bowl history. America's Team was back.

The next year, for the first time in Super Bowl history, the same two teams met again. And Dallas won again, 30–10, handing Buffalo their fourth straight Super Bowl loss. The Cowboys had won back-to-back championships for the first time in their storied history.

The 49ers toppled the Cowboys in 1994, but the Cowboys were far from finished. The next year, they returned to the Super Bowl, beating Pittsburgh, giving Dallas three championships in four years. After almost a decade of devastation, the Cowboys had returned to their glory days.

SUPER BOWL XXVII
TOP TEN LIST

After losing four straight Super Bowls the Buffalo Bills were the butt of many jokes for many years. As John Madden said, the greatest gap in sports is between the winner and loser of a Super Bowl. Though they never won the Super Bowl, there was still no better team in the AFC for four straight years than the Bills. Here are ten great teams that fell just short of victory, yet were anything but losers.

1. Buffalo Bills (1991–1994): Lost four straight Super Bowls, but boasted five Hall of Famers.
2. Minnesota Vikings (1970–1978): Lost four Super Bowls, but sent four players to the Hall of Fame.
3. Denver Broncos (1987–1990): Lost three Super Bowls in four seasons, but they eventually had their moments with the Lombardi Trophy.
4. Dallas Cowboys (1975, 1978): Lost to Pittsburgh twice, but both Super Bowls were legendary.

5. New England Patriots (2008, 2012): Only miraculous, last-second catches caused their downfall in both Super Bowl losses to the Giants.

6. Seattle Seahawks (2015): One fatal offensive mistake at the goal line led to a turnover and prevented a title repeat.

7. Arizona Cardinals (2009): The Cards gave their fans a taste of the Super Bowl for the first time, but fell just short of victory.

8. Cincinnati Bengals (1989): Had a chance to win their first Super Bowl, but Joe Montana took them down in heartbreaking fashion in the fourth quarter.

9. Tennessee Titans (2000): Lost on the last play of the Super Bowl at the goal line. No losing team has ever come closer to winning.

10. Green Bay Packers (1998): A determined John Elway prevented the Packers from winning a second title under Favre's leadership.

SUPER BOWL XXXII FINALLY, A CHAMPION

DENVER BRONCOS VS. GREEN BAY PACKERS

There was no doubt by the end of the 1997 season that John Elway was a great quarterback, easily one of the best ever. He had a cannon for a right arm that was so powerful it looked like he could throw a football through a brick wall. He threw the ball so fast that even in heavy coverage he could complete a pass to a receiver quicker than a defender could react to knock the ball down. Elway was speedy on his feet, too. For years, defensive ends and linebackers cursed themselves for the times they thought they had Elway cornered, only to see him scramble and turn a dead end into a great play. He was also very strong compared to his counterparts. Some quarterbacks fell to the ground if a defender sneezed on them. Not Elway. He was six foot three, 220 pounds. Getting a hand on him didn't mean he was going down easily.

Most of all, Elway had the leadership. Everyone, especially the Cleveland Browns, remembered "The Drive," when Elway drove Denver 98 yards in the 1987 AFC Championship Game for the tying score. They remembered Elway taking the Broncos to the Super Bowl in 1986, 1987, and 1989.

What was in doubt, however, was whether John Elway would ever win a Super Bowl. In the first six years of his career, Elway went to the Super Bowl three times.

And each time he got there, he got thumped.

Super Bowl XXI: Giants 39, Broncos 20.

Super Bowl XXII: Washington 42, Broncos 10.

Super Bowl XXIV: 49ers 55, Broncos 10.

Ouch.

In the next six years, he hadn't returned once.

Maybe it wasn't meant to be, for one of the all-time great quarterbacks. Even great players have to understand that losing is so much more common than winning. After all, every season finishes with just one winner. Everyone else? They lose.

So when the Denver Broncos reached Super Bowl XXXII, Elway was thirty-seven years old and the sentimental favorite. The rumor was that Elway just might retire after the game. Fans began to imagine how fitting it would be if the great old quarterback finally won the championship after years of disappointment.

Everyone likes a fairy-tale ending.

Elway had as good a shot as he ever had, given the cast of players that surrounded him. This Broncos team was different from the others who had been humiliated in past Super Bowls, because they had a running game this time around. Terrell Davis, the great young running back, was a difference maker. In the old days, Elway had to make every play, every throw, because the Broncos had no balance. The addition of Davis allowed the running game to take some pressure off of Elway. Davis blended power and speed and a knack for always moving his feet forward. Davis was in his third year and had improved his rushing totals each year. In 1997, he rushed for 1,750 yards, an average of 115 yards a game, plus 15 touchdowns.

Still, the odds were against Denver, because they were playing the defending Super Bowl champion Green Bay Packers.

The Packers were the first dynasty of the NFL's television age during the 1960s, but after winning Super Bowl I and II, the Packers hadn't returned to the Super Bowl since.

Following thirty years of mediocrity, the Packers' revival rested on the brain of Ron Wolf, the general manager of the team, who traded with Atlanta for a young, brash, and talented quarterback named Brett Favre. Like Elway, Favre was blessed with a powerful arm—which earned him the nickname "The Gunslinger"—and the daring to make great plays as games wound down.

Even with a stellar quarterback, it took time for Green Bay to find success. Much like the Packers, the Dallas Cowboys had finally returned to glory after years of poor play, winning three of the previous four Super Bowls. So for three straight years, the Packers lost to Dallas in the playoffs. But then in 1996, Green Bay avoided Dallas when Carolina stunned the Cowboys in the NFC divisional round. The Packers defeated the Panthers and went on to beat the Patriots to win the Super Bowl for the first time since 1968.

In the playoffs, Green Bay had already beaten the other dynasty of the era, San Francisco, for three straight years. Finally, in Week 13 of the 1997 season, they beat Dallas, crushing them 45–17. They went 13-3 during the regular season and were now clearly the best team in the NFC.

The Packers had more talent than just Favre, but he was the guy who could make other players better, especially guys who weren't stars. The Packers' offense, with Favre, wide receivers Antonio Freeman and Robert Brooks, running back Dorsey Levens, and Pro Bowl tight end Mark Chmura, was second in the league in offense. The Packers' defense, anchored by the great defensive end Reggie White and the massive, 340-pound defensive tackle Gilbert Brown, was fifth, giving up just 17.8 points per game.

After taking down two dynasties in the 49ers and the Cowboys, the Packers were sixty minutes away from winning their second straight Super Bowl, just like Vince Lombardi's Packers had.

In Denver, there was so much on the line. The Broncos wanted to win for Elway, but they also wanted to win as an organization. Four times the Broncos had been to the Super Bowl and four times they'd lost, each time by at least 17 points. Everyone knew how bad Buffalo had felt after losing four Super Bowls in a row, but the Broncos risked being the first franchise in NFL history to lose *five* Super Bowls.

As if the Broncos weren't already under enough pressure, the conference they represented, the AFC, had been shelled in Super Bowls for the past fourteen years, having lost every single game since 1984, when the Raiders beat Washington 38–9. And the odds were against Denver, who were 11-point underdogs!

Was Green Bay really 11 points better than Denver?

Despite the perceived mismatch, the result was one of the best, most physical Super Bowls ever played. Football is a brutal game, full of big hits and violent collisions, but this Super Bowl was especially hard-hitting, both teams wanting to win bad. The Packers took the opening kick, and eight plays later, Favre hit Freeman for a 22-yard touchdown.

Denver stormed right back. After a couple of first downs, Davis broke free to his left for twenty-seven yards, his first big run of the day, moving the ball to the Packers' 14-yard line. Two plays later, Elway rushed for ten more down to the 2-yard line, leaping headfirst to the yard marker. Davis finished the drive by crashing through the middle into the end zone for a touchdown that tied the score.

Green Bay got the ball back, but two plays later Favre scrambled to avoid a blitz and was intercepted by Denver. The Broncos had the ball at the Green Bay 45-yard line. Davis plowed ahead for sixteen yards.

A few plays into the drive, the ball at the 10, Davis received a handoff and took a big hit. With 1:29 left in the first quarter, Davis already had 62 yards rushing and a touchdown. But after the hit, he sat on his knees in pain, wracked with a migraine so intense that it blurred his vision. He left the game, yet re-entered as a decoy, allowing Elway to finish the drive with a 1-yard touchdown run.

Denver, the big underdogs, led 14–7.

On the next drive, Broncos safety Steve Atwater crushed Favre, forcing him to cough up the ball. Denver recovered the fumble, kicked a field goal, and increased their lead to 17–7. Suddenly, the team who wasn't expected to win seemed to be in firm control.

But without Davis, who still wasn't well enough to carry the ball, Denver was a different, weaker team.

Green Bay ended the half with an eighteen-play drive and a touchdown pass. At halftime, Denver held a slight lead, 17–14.

Davis returned in the second half, yet still wasn't himself. On the first play of the half, he was hit by Packers defensive back Tyrone Williams and fumbled. Green Bay recovered the ball just shy of the red zone. A few plays later, they tied the game with a field goal, 17–17.

Halfway through the quarter, the hitting got even harder. With Davis feeling better and back in action, the Broncos drove the length of the field from their own 8-yard line. At Green Bay's 16-yard line, Elway began scrambling, running hard. With the first-down marker in sight, he leaped and was hit simultaneously by three Packers. The hits were so hard that he went spinning in the air like a helicopter!

Davis then powered into the end zone for his second touchdown, carrying linebacker Bernardo Harris on his back to bring the score to 24–17.

The Broncos were so close to the elusive championship. Excitement continued to build as Freeman fumbled the very next kickoff. Elway immediately went for the kill, throwing into the end zone, but safety Eugene Robinson intercepted the pass.

The game was far from over. Favre, with another chance, drove the Packers 78 yards for the tying score.

Heading into the fourth quarter, the game was tied 24–24.

There had never been an overtime game in Super Bowl history, but as the Green Bay and Denver defenses continued to beat up on the opposing offenses, the prospect began looking more and more likely.

Finally, the Green Bay defense, battered by Davis, weakened. He had missed an entire quarter, yet already had racked up over 100 yards rushing. A poor punt by the Packers gave Denver the ball near midfield, and a 15-yard facemask penalty on a carry by Davis put the Broncos in even better field position. On the sidelines and between plays, Reggie White, Gilbert Brown, and the rest of the Packers' defensive line were so tired they couldn't breathe. Elway took advantage of the winded Packers and completed a pass to Howard Griffith for 23 yards with 2:29 left. Davis continued to pound the ball downfield, running around the left end for 17 yards, all the way to the one. Then, through a dog-tired Green Bay defense, he punched in his third touchdown of the game, a Super Bowl record. Denver led 31–24 with 1:45 left.

Last chance for Green Bay. Could Favre, known for orchestrating comeback wins, tie the game? Green Bay moved the ball furiously all the way down to the Denver 31. After two incompletions Favre threw the ball in Brooks's direction, but Steve Atwater, the bruising Denver safety, ran so fast and hard to break up the play he ran full speed, helmet first, into Randy Hilliard, his own teammate. Both players were knocked out cold. Brooks was knocked flat, too.

Fourth down, 6 yards to go. Thirty-two seconds left in the game. One last chance for the Packers to win back-to-back Super Bowls. Denver rushed on a blitz and Favre tried to hit Chmura on a slant. As the fans held their breath, the pass was batted down by John Mobley.

Game over. Victory at last.

Strangely, the game that many thought would be the start of a Packers dynasty, similar to those of the 49ers and Cowboys before them, fell short of expectations. Under Favre, the Packers would never again reach a Super Bowl.

Yet for the Broncos, after fifteen years and three terrible Super Bowl defeats, John Elway had finally won his first championship. Davis rushed for 157 yards and 3 touchdowns and was named the game's Most Valuable Player. The Broncos were no longer just Super Bowl runner-ups. They were champions.

The following season, 1998, Davis rushed for an amazing 2,008 yards, clearly on his way to becoming one of the all-time great players. Then, a year later, in the prime of his career, he injured his knee severely. He tried to play for the next three years, but was never the same player. As the cruelest example of how brutal a sport football can be, the great Terrell Davis retired before he was thirty. But for his very short time in the NFL, there was perhaps no one better.

Davis and Elway had one last season together, though. Contrary to expectations, Elway did not retire after finally winning his first championship. Now that he'd gotten a taste of victory, his days of winning weren't over just yet. The next year, the Broncos nearly went undefeated, reached the Super Bowl, and won again, beating Atlanta. Finally, at age thirty-eight, with two Super Bowl victories under his belt, Elway retired, and walked away from the game. His heartbreaking losses of the past were but a memory, and Elway finished off his career by cementing his legacy as an elite player. He would always be remembered as a champion.

SUPER BOWL XXXII
TOP TEN LIST

n Super Bowl XXXII John Elway finally won a title, and although Terrell Davis stole the show, the game played host to a faceoff between two Hall of Fame–bound quarterbacks. It doesn't happen often, but when it does, such matchups demand to be remembered. Here are ten great matchups between great leading men.

1. Super Bowl X: Pittsburgh Steelers' Terry Bradshaw vs. Dallas Cowboys' Roger Staubach: Bradshaw wins his second title.
2. Super Bowl XI: Oakland Raiders' Ken Stabler vs. Minnesota Vikings' Fran Tarkenton: Stabler, who passed away in 2015, is not a Hall of Famer, but he's still remembered as a big-game player.
3. Super Bowl XIII: A rematch between Pittsburgh Steelers' Terry Bradshaw and Dallas Cowboys'

Staubach: The Steelers win again, their third victory under Bradshaw.

4. Super Bowl XVIII: San Francisco 49ers' Joe Montana vs. Miami Dolphins' Dan Marino: Montana rolls for his second Super Bowl win. Marino goes on to set numerous passing records, yet never returns to the Big Game.

5. Super Bowl XXIV: San Francisco 49ers' Joe Montana vs. Denver Broncos' John Elway: Despite the big names featured, it was a blowout as Montana reigned supreme again.

6. Super Bowl XXXII: Denver Broncos' John Elway vs. Green Bay Packers' Brett Favre: There were certainly fireworks in the passing game, but Terrell Davis ended up stealing the show.

7. Super Bowl XXVII: Dallas Cowboys' Troy Aikman vs. Buffalo Bills' Jim Kelly: Both players wound up in the Hall of Fame, but Aikman and the Cowboys handled Buffalo easily.

8. Super Bowl XXXVI: New England Patriots' Tom Brady vs. St. Louis Rams' Kurt Warner: No one knew it at the time, but Brady's legacy of greatness began that day, as he earned his first

Super Bowl victory. Warner was a former league and Super Bowl MVP.

9. Super Bowl XLIV: Indianapolis Colts' Peyton Manning vs. New Orleans Saints' Drew Brees: Manning was the bigger name, but Brees and his Saints won their first Super Bowl in an emotional game for a team whose city had been devastated by Hurricane Katrina.

10. Super Bowl XLIX: New England Patriots' Tom Brady vs. Seattle Seahawks' Russell Wilson: A pure classic, in which Brady was on the verge of yet another heartbreaking loss until Wilson threw a shocking interception in the final seconds.

SUPER BOWL XXXIV THE GREATEST SHOW ON TURF

St. Louis Rams vs. Tennessee Titans

Baseball is a game bound by tradition. The actual rules of the game really haven't changed very much since the late 1800s. The rule revisions that have fundamentally affected how the game is played—changing the ball in 1920 and lowering the mound after the 1968 season to create more offense, for example—happen so rarely that the game of baseball as it's played today is very similar to the game that was played in 1930.

Football, however, could not be more different. The

biggest changes in football have been to the rules, and by the late 1990s, the NFL had done virtually everything it could to keep defensive players from hitting quarterbacks and holding wide receivers. Think for a minute, that in 1933, when running the ball was the primary means of offense, Cincinnati did not throw for a *single* touchdown pass. Neither did Pittsburgh in 1945. That would never, ever happen today.

Nobody quite knew what the results of the rule changes would be. We'd seen glimpses of the possibilities thanks to the Raiders of the 1960s and the Chargers of the '70s, both featuring prolific downfield passing attacks. And we'd seen the big-time scoring potential of Bill Walsh's West Coast offense.

But what the St. Louis Rams produced in 1999 was unlike anything anyone in football had ever seen. The Rams had four dynamic receivers in Isaac "Ike" Bruce, Torry Holt, Ricky Proehl, and Az-Zahir Hakim. Bruce and Holt were the showstoppers, but Proehl and Hakim were dangerous in their own right, especially because defenses had to spend their time focusing on the other two Rams receivers. In total, the four combined for almost 3,000 receiving yards and twenty-six touchdown catches.

In the old days, defenses only had to worry about the two top offensive players on great teams. The Rams ripped that model to shreds, because not only did they throw four great receivers at a defense, their best player on offense was their running back, Marshall Faulk.

In San Francisco, the old 49ers dynasty had the great Roger Craig, the first player in history to net 1,000 rushing yards and 1,000 receiving yards in a single season. Faulk could not only catch the ball as well as Craig, but he was also one of the greatest runners of all time. Marshall Faulk was so good that any time he touched the ball, he had a chance to score a touchdown. In 1999, he surpassed Craig, finishing the season with more than 1,300 rushing yards and over 1,000 receiving yards. He averaged 5.5 yards per carry and scored twelve touchdowns for the offense. And *still*, Faulk was not the offense's MVP that season.

The Rams benefitted from playing indoors on turf, which meant they did not need to worry about the wind, rain, snow, or any bad weather conditions when they played home games. It was like a track meet with a football.

Dick Vermeil, the coach of the Rams, had a plan to attack the new NFL, where passing was king. In order to stretch out defenses, he would take advantage of the speed of his wideouts and Faulk in the passing game, and when defenders tried to bottle up his receivers, Vermeil would unleash Faulk and his superior rushing ability.

There was only one question: who was the quarterback with all those weapons at his disposal?

The quarterback was Kurt Warner, a guy no one had ever heard of, *a guy no team wanted*. At one point, Warner played in the Arena Football League, which is more like a league for amateurs rather than professional football players. Arena games aren't even played eleven-on-eleven. It's arcade football.

Then, Warner went to play in an experimental league called NFL Europe, which was created by the NFL as a way to expand the appeal of the league globally and to build a minor league of sorts. But while Warner was in Europe, most American fans, coaches, and players didn't get a chance to see him in action.

Lucky for the Rams, Vermeil was one of the few who had seen Warner play, and he had a hunch about the quarterback—a hunch that paid off gloriously for the Rams. When Vermeil named Warner a starter, the Rams went on a tear. In his first full season with the team, they went 13-3, scored an incredible 526 points, and totaled 30 points or more in twelve out of sixteen games. Warner completed 65% of his passes that year for 4,353 yards and forty-one touchdowns. This guy that almost no one in the NFL had heard of was named MVP of the league!

Who would've thought that the Rams would be the team to dismantle opponents week after week? Certainly not their hated rivals, the 49ers. Yet the Rams destroyed them, crushing them in both match-ups, including a 42–20 wipeout in Week 5. It was sweet victory for the St. Louis faithful.

The Rams had been around since the 1940s, ever since they played in Los Angeles. They moved to St. Louis in 1994 and hadn't had much success before 1999. The Rams teams prior to the Warner era were good but not great. They had gone to the Super Bowl once, in 1979, and lost to Pittsburgh. They'd been especially bad since moving to St. Louis, failing to finish higher than third place in their division in any season. After falling to last place in the 1998 season, the Rams turned the tables and finished in first just a year later.

Suddenly they were the hottest team in football, and one of the best offensive teams the league had ever seen. The Rams, nicknamed "The Greatest Show on Turf," beat teams by a league-best average of 17.5 points per game.

Following a spectacular regular season, it was no surprise that the Rams demolished Minnesota in the divisional playoffs. The NFC Championship game wasn't quite so easy. St. Louis faced a stiff test in Tampa Bay, one of the toughest defensive teams in the league. For the first time all season, the Rams looked human. They scored just 11 points, their lowest single-game total of the season, but their defense held and they won, 11–6. For the first time in twenty years, the Rams were going to the Super Bowl.

They would play the Tennessee Titans in Super Bowl XXXIV, which was something of a coincidence because, like the Rams, the Titans had moved as well. They were once the Houston Oilers, an original member of the AFL. Owner Bud Adams had moved the Oilers to Nashville and changed their name.

They met in Atlanta's Georgia Dome, and the Rams

were favored. The game was set to take place indoors, which would play to the speed of the Rams, but the Titans had magic themselves. They had played and fought through the tough AFC with a more traditional approach: power football.

Tennessee had good receivers like Derrick Mason and Kevin Dyson, and an effective tight end in Frank Wycheck. They were all solid contributors, but by no means superstars. The true leaders of the Titans' offense were Eddie George, a powerful running back from Ohio State who combined speed and a whole lot of strength, and quarterback Steve McNair. McNair was not flashy like Warner, but he was a leader and a winner, who used his legs and throwing arm to his advantage. The Titans also had a dependable group of defenders. Chief among them was defensive end Jevon Kearse, who recorded 14.5 sacks and 8 fumbles in his rookie season, and was named a Pro Bowler and the Defensive Rookie of the Year.

Talented though they were, Tennessee hadn't beaten up on the rest of the league all year long like St. Louis had. The Rams were the overwhelming favorite. As expected, the Titans were outplayed early on. Tennessee's offense could barely move the ball against St. Louis's defense. They punted on all but one of their first-half possessions. On the only drive where they were able to move the ball downfield, they missed a 47-yard field goal on their way to putting up zero points in the first half.

The Rams, on the other hand, were able to move the ball into scoring range on every single drive in the first half. The only problem was that they couldn't finish the job and put the ball in the end zone! Yet they still managed to score three field goals, and out-gain Tennessee by 205 yards in the first half. Despite the apparent lopsidedness of the matchup, St. Louis led by a modest margin, 9–0, at halftime. The game, amazingly, was still up for grabs.

Both offenses started to heat up in the second half. Right out of the gate, the Titans moved the ball to the Rams' 29-yard line, but they failed to capitalize, missing yet another 47-yard field goal attempt on a blocked kick by defensive back Todd Lyght. After being kept out of the end zone in the first half, St. Louis had no such trouble in the second half. On their first drive of the half, after the missed field goal, Warner went right to work and hit Ike Bruce for a 31-yard gain. A few plays later, the Rams finally found the end zone, with a 9-yard touchdown strike to Bruce.

Down 16–0, the Titans were in dire straits unless they could get their offense back on track. It was time for Steve McNair and Eddie George to step up or go home with the taste of losing in their mouths.

On the strength of McNair's leadership and George's legs, the Titans made a furious second-half charge. Halfway through the third quarter, Tennessee turned up the gears and set Eddie George loose on the Rams. He rushed five times, and McNair completed two passes to advance to just outside of the red zone. On the next play, McNair proved that George wasn't the only Titan who could use his legs. He broke away from the line of scrimmage and ran for twenty-three yards, bringing Tennessee within range of the goal line. Two plays later, George scored a 1-yard touchdown. After a failed two-point conversion attempt, the Titans were down 16–6.

Entering the fourth quarter, the Titans' juices were flowing. The defense responded by forcing the Rams to punt. On the ensuing drive, the Tennessee quarterback showed the fans why he'd earned the nickname "Air" McNair. After a couple of 20-yard completions to tight end Jackie Harris and wide receiver Isaac Byrd, Eddie George cakewalked into the end zone once more to bring the Titans within a field goal, 16–13.

Momentum had swung in favor of Tennessee, and a demoralized Warner couldn't find any room to work with on the next drive. The Rams went three and out, and the Titans returned the punt to just shy of midfield. A few gains later, the Titans were in field goal range. With the game clock winding down, Tennessee's kicker, Del Greco, had a chance to tie the game, having already missed his first two field goal attempts.

Would he miss his third at a crucial moment?

With all eyes on Del Greco, he launched a kick that sailed through the uprights, and the game was tied with 2:12 remaining.

The pressure appeared to be getting to the Rams. Could they come all this way, to the Super Bowl, the team that scored 500 points in the regular season, and not even score 20 points?

Tied at 16, Warner dropped back to pass and threw deep down the right sideline to Bruce, who caught the ball, cut between two panicked Titans defenders, and ran 80 yards for a touchdown.

That was the Rams: tie game, but then one play for 80 yards changed everything.

The Titans' offense wasn't built for that sort of play, but McNair was a winner.

With 1:48 left to play, it was touchdown or bust for Tennessee.

McNair went to work. He hit Dyson for 9 yards and Wycheck for 7 more. Then the rush came and McNair scrambled away from the attack, gaining 12 yards. While he was running, the Rams cornerback Dré Bly grabbed McNair by the face mask, which added a 15-yard penalty to the run. That put the ball in Rams territory. Filled with nervous energy, the Rams became mistake prone. They committed yet another penalty, to put the ball at their 40-yard line with fifty-nine seconds left.

Bly almost made up for his mistake and ended the game, stepping in front of a pass intended for Mason, but the ball sailed through his arms. As the clock wound down, the Titans marched slowly but surely toward the end zone. On third and five from the 26, McNair dropped back and was nearly knocked down by two defenders, but he managed to stay on his feet and find Dyson for 16 more, moving the ball to the

10-yard line. With six seconds remaining, McNair stopped the clock, burning Tennessee's last time-out.

There had never been a Super Bowl that went to overtime, but the Titans were closing in on tying the game before time expired.

Time for one last play.

McNair dropped back and saw Dyson slant toward the end zone.

He was open!

McNair hit him at the 5. Dyson sped toward the end zone, a touchdown well within his sights. But at the last second, Rams linebacker Mike Jones caught Dyson at the ankles. Dyson lunged forward, trying to stretch the ball over the goal line . . . but the ball hit the ground at the 1-yard line.

The clock struck zero.

The game was over.

Ironically, the Rams, known all season for their offense, won the Super Bowl on a defensive play. However, for most of the game, the offense had stolen the show. Warner threw for over 400 yards, and Bruce and Holt both had over 100 yards receiving. St. Louis's air attack was on full display that fateful Super Bowl Sunday. On the backs of their offense and one timely defensive play, the Rams had won their first championship in the Super Bowl era and their first since 1950. A nail-biter to the very end, Super Bowl XXXIV would go down as one of the greatest Super Bowl finishes of all time.

SUPER BOWL XXXIV
TOP TEN LIST

I t might feel like your favorite football teams have been around forever, but football is still a business, and businesses are often forced to relocate. You might not realize that the St. Louis Rams were once the Los Angeles Rams. Here are ten teams that started in a different city or were once known by a different name.

1. Oakland Raiders: Played in Oakland from 1960 to 1981, moved to Los Angeles from 1982 to 1994, and returned to Oakland in 1995.

2. St. Louis Rams: Started in Cleveland in 1937, moved to Los Angeles in 1946, then on to St. Louis in 1995.

3. Indianapolis Colts: Were the famed Baltimore Colts from 1953 to 1982, and then moved to Indianapolis in the middle of the night for the 1983 season.

4. Arizona Cardinals: Started in Chicago in 1920,

moved to St. Louis in 1960, and then once more to Phoenix in 1988.

5. New England Patriots: Known as the Boston Patriots from 1960 to 1970.

6. Pittsburgh Steelers / Philadelphia Eagles: Merged during World War II and changed their name to the "Steagles."

7. Tennessee Titans: Played as the Houston Oilers from 1960 to 1996, then played as the Tennessee Oilers for two years, and finally changed their name to the Titans in 1999.

8. Washington: Began as the Boston Braves in 1932 before moving to Washington, DC, in 1937.

9. Kansas City Chiefs: Began in 1960 as the Dallas Texans before moving to Kansas City in 1963.

10. Baltimore Ravens: Believe it or not, the Ravens were once the Cleveland Browns. Browns owner at the time Art Modell decided to relocate the Browns to Baltimore, but the NFL insisted the team name remain in Cleveland. So the players and coaches moved and a new team name was chosen—the Ravens. The city of Cleveland was without a team until a new version of the Browns could be developed, a period of four years.

SUPER BOWL XXXVI
AN UNLIKELY
DYNASTY IS BORN

NEW ENGLAND PATRIOTS VS.
ST. LOUIS RAMS

For the first thirty-three years of their existence, the New England Patriots were laughed at. They were a team that was often on the wrong end of highlight reels, the one getting run over by the more talented teams in the league. They were the team that O. J. Simpson, the great running back of the Buffalo Bills, humiliated because their defense could never stop him. They were the team the Miami Dolphins beat up on year after year. From 1967 to 1986, the Patriots lost every game they played in Miami. They were the team plagued by bad fortune the few times they put together good seasons, like in 1976, when they lost to the Oakland Raiders in the playoffs on a bad call by the officials. Or in 1978, when their coach, Chuck Fairbanks, was suspended right before the playoffs for accepting a head coaching position with the University of Colorado in the final week of the regular season. The list of unfortunate events goes on and on. In 1981, the Patriots were finally showcased on *Monday Night Football*, but the fans were so rowdy that the town of Foxborough banned the team from playing *Monday Night Football* at home again until a new owner appealed the decision in 1995. And when they *finally* made the Super Bowl in 1985, New England got demolished 46–10 by the Chicago Bears.

In 1993, it seemed as though the Patriots had turned over a new leaf. Robert Kraft, a season-ticket holder since 1971 (when they were still known as the Boston Patriots), bought the team and immediately hired Bill Parcells, the two-time Super Bowl–winning coach of the New York Giants. Parcells was the most accomplished coach the Patriots had ever hired, and brought immediate credibility to a team known for losing.

Along with the acquisition of a prominent coach, New England began recruiting promising players through the draft. To fill the role of quarterback, they drafted rocket-armed Drew Bledsoe out of Washington State. Bledsoe was joined by the quiet, talented running back Curtis Martin, great young defensive backs Lawyer Milloy and Ty Law, defensive end Willie McGinest, and wide receivers Troy Brown and Terry Glenn. The Patriots had so much young talent, they appeared poised to be a good—if not great—team for a long, long time.

Then, the Patriots turned into the Patriots, as bad luck struck when everything seemed to be going their way. In 1996, they surprisingly reached the Super Bowl. The Patriots played hard, but despite their best efforts, they lost the game badly, 35–21. To make matters worse, after the season, Parcells quit the team to coach the rival New York Jets.

For the next five years the Patriots underachieved, never quite living up to the promise of their youth and talent. Martin followed Parcells to the Jets. Glenn went to the Packers. After the 1999 season, Kraft hired an old Parcells disciple, Bill Belichick, as the new head coach, hoping to rebuild the Patriots. Belichick had served as the Jets' defensive coordinator under Parcells, and had accepted the Jets head coaching position when Parcells stepped down in 1999. However, in a bizarre set of events, just one day after accepting the position with New York, Belichick audibled and decided to leave the Jets to become head coach of New England. The Jets were wounded and the Patriots were bolstered.

It was a decision that would ultimately change the course of football history.

In Belichick's first year, 2000, the Patriots went 5-11. In his second year, New England appeared to be heading for disaster. In Week 2, when the Patriots were home against the Jets, Bledsoe dropped back to pass, and ran along the right sideline before being hit like a sledgehammer by Jets linebacker Mo Lewis.

Bledsoe would be out indefinitely, having severed a blood vessel in his chest. At one point, Bledsoe's injury was considered life threatening.

The Patriots' season was seemingly over. After two games, both losses. Bledsoe had been the present and the future of the Patriots, having just signed a contract worth nearly $100 million. Belichick had no choice but to start a little-known backup named Tom Brady. Brady, a sixth-round pick, 199th overall in the 2000 draft, had just barely earned a spot on the team.

Brady's professional start came against the game's rising young star, Peyton Manning, and the Patriots won 44–13. The victory came mainly on the backs of New England's running backs, who combined for 177 rushing yards. The Patriots went on to split the first eight games of the season and were 5-4 on the season when St. Louis came to Foxborough for a Sunday-night clash.

The Rams entered the game at 8-1 and were the most fearsome offensive team in the league. The Patriots were beginning to play well, but were by no means expected to be able to compete with the Greatest Show on Turf.

The Patriots took a 10–7 second-quarter lead before the Rams stormed downfield and scored right before the half, when Kurt Warner hit Marshall Faulk to make it 14–10. The Rams went up 24–10 in the second half, before the Patriots scored midway through the fourth. That was as close as New England would come to catching St. Louis.

The Rams won, 24–17. Warner threw for 401 yards in a game where St. Louis ran twenty-two more offensive plays than New England. The numbers were clearly in the Rams' favor, but after the game, their coach Mike Martz said the Patriots hit his guys harder and gave his offense more trouble than any team they'd played all year.

The Patriots were 5-5 on the year, and while no one likes losing, Belichick and Brady both recognized something very important after the Rams game: if St. Louis was the best team in football, the Patriots weren't that far away from being the best, because the Rams did not frighten them one bit.

The Patriots did not lose a game for the rest of the regular season, surprisingly going 11-5, even securing a home game for the divisional playoffs. Despite his inexperience, Brady had emerged as more than just a formidable backup—he'd staked his claim as the team's starter.

There was, however, one problem. Drew Bledsoe was healthy again, and he wanted his job back. The unspoken rule in sports is that players aren't supposed to lose their jobs to injury. When a player is healthy, he normally earns the right to become the starter again.

Belichick felt differently. The Patriots were playing well. Brady had shown leadership. The team was on a winning streak. He had made up his mind: the job belonged to Brady now.

The AFC divisional game was against the Oakland Raiders, the legendary team that had tortured the Patriots in the past, when a roughing-the-passer penalty against New England defensive end Ray "Sugar Bear" Hamilton ended New England's chances in the 1976 playoffs. The Raiders wound up winning that game and going on to win the Super Bowl.

The game was played in a blizzard, and neither team could move the ball, but the Raiders outplayed the Patriots for most of the game. The snow came down so hard the field was a sheet of white. The line markers couldn't be cleared fast enough before more snow fell to re-cover them.

The Raiders took a 13–3 lead into the fourth quarter, but the Patriots kept hope alive when Brady rushed into the end zone to make it 13–10. With little time remaining on the clock, Brady got the ball back and drove the Patriots into Raiders territory. Now within striking distance, Brady snapped the ball and motioned to throw when his old Michigan teammate Charles Woodson came on a blitz and knocked the ball loose. Woodson's teammate, linebacker Greg Biekert, picked up the loose ball.

Raiders' ball. Under two minutes left. Game over.

Oakland celebrated on the sidelines. The Patriots' surprise season was over. Patriots fans were stunned, and slowly began walking up the steps toward the exits.

But on the field, the referees huddled.

After discussing the call, they went and looked at the replay.

What were they looking at? The play was clearly a fumble.

Or was it?

After nearly ten minutes of reviewing the play, the officials emerged and declared that even though Brady had been bringing the ball down to his waist, his arm had been in the process of a throwing motion. Therefore, it wasn't a fumble, but an incomplete pass. The rule was called the "tuck rule," and it meant the game wasn't over after all. It was still the Patriots' ball.

The season was still alive!

The crowd went insane!

The Raiders were furious, then deflated. If the ball had been completely tucked into Brady's body before he lost possession, it would have been a fumble.

There was still the matter of getting into field goal range. Brady threw pass after pass to move the Pats into scoring range. Then the difficult task of kicking a 45-yard, game-tying field goal through the blizzard fell to New England kicker Adam Vinatieri.

With the winds howling, Vinatieri nailed the kick, and the Patriots and Raiders were tied. Overtime.

The Patriots won the toss, immediately marched downfield, and Vinatieri did it again, kicking the game-winner in overtime.

16–13, New England. Game over—for real this time. New England should have been beaten, but they weren't, saved by the rule book—and maybe a little karma from decades ago, when the Raiders had beaten them in a similarly controversial manner.

They went to Pittsburgh and, in another close game, stunned the Steelers in the AFC championship, 24–17, and the legend of Tom Brady grew. Even Bledsoe, now a backup, entered the game after Brady took a hard shot in the second quarter, and threw a touchdown to David Patten.

The Patriots, who started the season 0-2, whose starting quarterback was severely injured, who got a second chance in the snow against Oakland, were now in the Super Bowl to play the best team in football: the St. Louis Rams.

The Rams had won the Super Bowl two years earlier. They were the only team in the history of the NFL to score 500 points in three straight seasons. They had already beaten the Patriots in the regular season. They were 14-point favorites to win, the biggest gap between Super Bowl teams ever.

The Rams finished 14-2 on the year. After destroying Green Bay in the NFC divisional round, they narrowly escaped Philadelphia to reach the Super Bowl. The cast of players was largely the same as the Super Bowl championship team that had beaten Tennessee two years earlier. Kurt Warner was the great quarterback, and Marshall Faulk the deadly rusher who could catch as well as he could run. The dangerous receivers, Torry Holt, Isaac Bruce, Ricky Proehl, and Az-Zahir Hakim, surrounded the defense on all sides.

The Patriots came out hitting. That was the strategy.

The Rams receivers liked catching the ball and rolling to the ground, so Belichick instructed his defenders to try to hit them first. The same was true for Warner. The plan was to rush Warner up the middle in order to throw him off his game.

The Rams took an early 3–0 lead, but then the Patriots, the huge underdogs who were supposed to be intimidated by the big stage of the Super Bowl, went to work. Patriots defensive back Terrell Buckley intercepted Warner and ran 47 yards for a touchdown. Then, with thirty-six seconds left in the first half, Brady hit Patten on the same pass pattern Bledsoe had used against the Steelers, and it was 14–3 at halftime.

What was happening? The Greatest Show on Turf was being grounded, indoors, by the Patriots?

The Patriots intercepted Warner again and that led to another field goal. With one quarter left, the Patriots led, 17–3.

Over the regular season, the Rams scored 503 points. They had Faulk. They had Holt. They had Bruce and Warner. It was time to turn up the heat.

Warner worked fast, hitting Bruce for 15 yards and Faulk for another 7. He found Hakim for 14, and kept throwing bull's-eyes, connecting with tight end Ernie Conwell and Faulk for another 22. With under eleven minutes left in the fourth quarter and down by 2 touchdowns, Warner dropped back and Patriots defensive end Roman Phifer caught Warner, knocking the ball loose at New England's 3-yard line. Cornerback Tebucky Jones picked up the loose ball and ran 97 yards for another touchdown.

The score was 24–3, and the Patriots were just minutes away from defying the odds—until everyone noticed the yellow flag on the play. Willie McGinest was called for defensive holding. The touchdown didn't count.

With new life, Warner ran a quarterback sneak up the middle to bring St. Louis within a touchdown.

Here came the Rams, down only a touchdown.

The Patriots went three-and-out on their next possession.

With 7:44 left, down 17–10, Warner moved the Rams to the Patriots' 38-yard line, but got no farther, and St. Louis was forced to punt the ball with 3:44 left.

One sustained drive could end the game. The Rams were relying on their defense to get a quick stop and give their offense one more opportunity to force the game to go to overtime. The Patriots had the ball at their 20, but they could not move the football. Three plays, no first down. New England punted once again, giving the most dangerous offense in football another chance to tie the game. With 1:51 left, trailing 17–10, St. Louis had excellent field position, starting off the drive from their own 45-yard line. Warner showed just how great the Greatest Show on Turf really was. He hit Hakim for 18 yards on a nifty crossing route. Then, Warner threw to backup receiver Yo Murphy for 11 more. He capped off the drive with a pass to Proehl down the sideline for 26 yards . . . Touchdown! Tie game.

The Rams were back. Belichick knew what everyone in America knew: if the Rams got the ball back again, the Patriots wouldn't be able to stop them, not after the way Warner had found his stride at the end of the fourth quarter. If New England ran out the clock and the game went into overtime, the Rams might do to them what the Patriots had done to the Raiders: take the ball downfield and score.

So Belichick trusted his young quarterback, Tom Brady, to win the game in regulation.

With 1:21 left on the clock, the Patriots ran the ensuing kickoff back to their own 17-yard line. Throwing caution to the wind, Brady launched a passing attack. He started off the drive by connecting with running back J. R. Redmond twice, once for 5 yards, and then again for 8 yards.

The Patriots were going for the win against the premiere team in the league, on the biggest stage in sports, with a guy who hadn't ever played a full season.

On television, the famous broadcaster, former coach, and video game emperor John Madden said "I don't like what the Patriots are doing." They were being too reckless. The expected, safe course of action was to run the clock out and try to win it in overtime rather than risk a turnover. One mistake could give the Rams the ball and the win.

But Brady, Belichick, and the rest of the Patriots weren't interested in what was safe or expected. They wanted to win and win now. Brady hit Redmond for 11 more, and with forty seconds left, New England was at their own 41, inching closer to field goal range.

Madden changed his tune. "You know what?" he said to the millions of viewers watching at home. "I kinda like what the Patriots are doing."

Brady kept on firing. After an incompletion, he found Troy Brown on a crossing route for 23 yards, which put the Patriots in Rams territory. The Patriots had enough time to run one more play before stopping the clock and putting the game in Vinatieri's hands. Brady made good use of it: The Patriots picked up 6 more yards on a short pass to tight end Jermaine Wiggins. Brady spiked the ball to stop the clock. With seven seconds remaining and the ball on the Rams' 31-yard line, the Patriots were looking at a long field goal.

Vinatieri came onto the field. He had tied the Raiders game on a clutch kick into the wind, with buckets full of snow falling from the sky.

He'd won that same game with a field goal in overtime.

Now, he stood waiting to kick a 48-yarder to give the Patriots their first-ever Super Bowl.

And he nailed it. Right through the middle.

Patriots 20, Rams 17.

A year earlier, Brady was just a guy with a clipboard, nothing but a backup quarterback nobody knew. Just a fourth-stringer who'd worked his way up to second in the depth chart. Now, he was a Super

Bowl champion, pulling off arguably the biggest upset in NFL history. He was named Super Bowl MVP. His idol was Joe Montana, the great 49er who won four Super Bowls. Now, Brady had one of his own.

Madden used to say that the greatest gap in sports is between the winner and loser of a Super Bowl. The Rams, the high-scoring team on their way to becoming the next dynasty, never even won a second Super Bowl. They are still waiting to return to the Big Game.

The Patriots, meanwhile, saw their entire history change. The good fortune of the snow game led to a championship and they took advantage. In a Super Bowl where a dynasty was expected to be born, a twist of fate occurred—a dynasty was indeed born, just not the one anyone was expecting. New England immediately went from losers to winners, the old history forgotten. A new chapter was about to be written that no one would ever forget.

SUPER BOWL XXXVI
TOP TEN LIST

In 2001, as a replacement starter, Tom Brady shocked the league with his performance. After all, it was only an injury to Drew Bledsoe that gave him the job in the first place. But the Super Bowl is a special place, and so often one player picks the biggest game of the year to have the biggest game of his life. Here are ten of the greatest surprise performances in Super Bowl history.

1. Timmy Smith, Washington: After running for only 126 yards the entire 1987 regular season, he rushed for 204 yards in Super Bowl XXII against Denver.
2. Chris Matthews, Seattle Seahawks: He did not catch a pass during the regular season, but caught four for 109 yards in Super Bowl XLIX against New England.
3. Phil Simms, New York Giants: A starter and a

solid contributor, he elevated his game to new
heights by completing 22 of 25 passes in Super
Bowl XXI against Denver.

4. Doug Williams, Washington: A journeyman
    quarterback who threw 4 touchdowns in the
    second quarter of an unexpected 42–10 rout of
    Denver in Super Bowl XXII.

5. Malcolm Smith, Seattle Seahawks: A lesser-
    known member of Seattle's famed Legion of
    Boom defense, but he recorded an interception
    and a fumble recovery on the way to being named
    the MVP of Super Bowl XLVIII against Denver.

6. Jim Plunkett, Oakland Raiders: Another
    journeyman quarterback, Plunkett rejuvenated
    his career with Oakland. Won Super Bowl XV
    MVP against Philadelphia.

7. Matt Snell, New York Jets: All eyes were on Joe
    Namath in Super Bowl III, but Snell ran for 121
    yards against the Colts.

8. Willie Parker, Pittsburgh Steelers: The bigger
    names in the game were Ben Roethlisberger and
    Hines Ward, but Parker ran for 93 yards against
    Seattle in Super Bowl XL and helped lead his
    team to victory.

9. Deion Branch, New England Patriots: Tom Brady was the MVP, but Branch caught 10 passes for 143 yards and a touchdown in Super Bowl XXXVIII against Carolina.

10. Hakeem Nicks, New York Giants: Eli Manning was the MVP, but like Branch, Hakeem Nicks played an important role in the victory, catching 10 passes for 109 yards in Super Bowl XLVI.

SUPER BOWL XXXVIII AND THEN THERE WERE TWO . . .

NEW ENGLAND PATRIOTS VS. CAROLINA PANTHERS

For decades, the NFL, and especially the Super Bowl, revolved around dynasties. The imagination of the game had always been dominated by those few teams who ranked at the top of the standings every year, the ones who held the trophies at season's end. Teams like Dallas, Pittsburgh, Oakland, San Francisco, and Green Bay.

Now in a new century, the NFL had been attempting to change its rules to give more teams a chance to be successful. In 1994, a salary cap was implemented.

Through this new financial rule, the league limited the total amount of money that could be spent on player salaries. This change prevented individual teams from adding all the best players and becoming super-teams, like the old 49ers dynasty. Never again would two Hall of Fame–level quarterbacks like Joe Montana and Steve Young play on the same team.

In the old days, when a team reached the Super Bowl for the first time, it was normal for them to get demolished by one of the old guard. Denver first reached the Super Bowl in 1977. Dallas killed them. The Rams reached the game in 1979. The Steelers stomped on them. The Eagles finally reached the Super Bowl in 1980. The Raiders . . . well, you get the idea.

So when the surprise team of the year, the Carolina Panthers, a team that had won just one game two years prior, reached Super Bowl XXXVIII in Houston against the New England Patriots, they were under-dogs by the old standards. Even so, the Panthers thought they had a great chance to win. The Panthers weren't even ten years old as a franchise, having joined the league as an expansion team in 1995. But the times had changed. The Buccaneers, another ex-pansion team, had proved as much the year before when they reached the Super Bowl for the first time, beating the Raiders so badly, 48–21, that it was hard to watch.

The Panthers were a weird team. They did not do anything traditionally well the way Super Bowl teams typically did. They ranked fifteenth in offense and tenth in defense. Usually, good teams that were average statistically won games off of turnovers, but their defense did not force a great number of interceptions or fumbles. They won games by an average of 1.3 points, hardly a machine.

The key to Carolina's success was simply their clutch, tough style of play. They went 11-5 in the regular season and beat Tampa Bay, the defending champions, twice. When they needed a big play, they had a strong-armed quarterback named Jake Delhomme, two fantastic deep-threat receivers, Muhsin Muhammad and Steve Smith, and a bruising running back, Stephen Davis. At a height of just 5' 9", Steve Smith possessed blazing speed and sure hands to make up for his lack of size. Though he wasn't of the standard build for a wide receiver, he had as much heart as any player on the field. Sometimes, it seemed as though Smith just *wanted* to win more than anyone else around and would put his body on the line to give his team the best chance to do so.

The Panthers were an efficient team that got hot at the right time. In the playoffs, they even beat two teams—Dallas and Philadelphia—that had defeated them during the regular season, and knocked off another top team, St. Louis, which was still considered an offensive powerhouse. Carolina flourished with its own brand of hard-hitting football. The Panthers somehow left their better-known opponents shaking their heads, wondering, "How did we lose?"

Well, after beating Philadelphia in the NFC title game, the Panthers were heading to the Super Bowl.

Just two years earlier, the Patriots had been the underdogs, shocking the Rams—and fans across America—by winning the Super Bowl. Now, there was no doubt that Tom Brady was one of the best quarterbacks in football. What he did in taking the Patriots to the Super Bowl against the Rams was not a matter of luck—New England's return to the Super Bowl for the second time in three seasons was proof. This Patriots team might have been the best in franchise history.

Despite the Patriots' immense talent, coach Bill

Belichick did not like the energy of his squad during the preseason, so he shook up the club by releasing strong safety Lawyer Milloy. Milloy, one of the great Patriots who'd played on two Super Bowl teams, and served as team captain for three seasons, refused to take a pay cut and the two sides failed to come to an agreement.

The Patriot players were devastated, and it showed when they went to Buffalo on opening day and lost 31–0. But this team was way too good to simply give up following one shocking loss. After starting the season 2-2 they quickly regrouped, and the Patriots ripped off twelve straight wins. During the streak, they won big, beating Philadelphia 31–10, and they also hung tight and pulled off victories in close games. They posted three shutouts, including a payback win over Buffalo to end the season, beating the Bills by the same 31–0 score they lost by in Week 1. And though Brady had established himself as an elite quarterback, the Patriots didn't have a top running back or a major wide receiver to target. In fact, there wasn't a single runner or receiver on the team who racked up 1,000 yards on the season. Tom Brady led the show and he found great success running Belichick's offensive scheme, distributing the ball to many different players.

The playoffs were all about a dream matchup with Peyton Manning and Indianapolis, Brady's great rival. The Patriots had already beaten the Colts indoors in Indianapolis 38–34 in Week 13 of the regular season. The AFC title game was being played in the icy cold of Foxborough.

Manning was the league's most glamorous quarterback, and he was armed with dangerous weapons, including receivers Reggie Wayne and Marvin Harrison, the reliable running back Edgerrin James, and tight end Dallas Clark. He threw for thousands of yards and did so many commercials he was among the league's most recognizable players.

Despite the hype, Brady and the Patriots had proven to be Manning's Achilles' heel, having defeated Indianapolis in all three of their previous matchups. This was the first time the two monumental quarterbacks had faced off in the playoffs.

Just like in the first three games, New England was too much to handle for the Colts. Manning threw three interceptions and the Patriots won 24–14, securing their return trip to the Super Bowl.

During the week leading up to the Super Bowl, the Patriots receivers grew angrier by the day because of the attention Carolina rookie cornerback Ricky Manning Jr. received. Manning Jr. was having a terrific postseason, disrupting plays and making timely interceptions, and the media loved his story.

The game was played at Reliant Stadium in Houston, the first time that city had ever hosted a Super Bowl. From the opening kickoff, the Patriots played as if they wanted not only to win, but also to send every member of the Panthers to the hospital.

The first quarter was one of the hardest-hitting quarters in Super Bowl history. Neither team scored, but the Panthers barely gained another yard for the rest of the quarter after their first possession. The only scoring opportunity came on a Vinatieri field goal opportunity, but it missed the mark.

The second quarter was much like the first, until both teams finally broke the scoring silence. The Patriots struck first. Delhomme had just one passing completion in the first quarter, and having already been sacked three times, coughed up the ball at the Panthers' 20-yard line. From there, it took New England just four plays to find the end zone as Brady connected with Deion Branch for a 5-yard touchdown.

The Panthers, determined not to fall behind after holding their own throughout the first quarter, had just as easy a time scoring on their next possession. The only difference was that they started on their own 5-yard line. The eight-play, 95-yard drive ended on a long 39-yard touchdown pass to Steve Smith.

After trading touchdowns, the Patriots came right back and completed a huge drive of their own. They went 78 yards and regained the lead on a Brady touchdown pass.

With very little time remaining in the first half, the Panthers got the ball back near midfield after New England, intending to catch Carolina off-guard, launched a poor squib kick. After a long run by Stephen Davis surprised the Patriots' defense, who were expecting a pass, Carolina's kicker, John Kasay, catapulted a 50-yard field goal through the uprights, to cut the Patriots' lead to 14–10 at the half.

In the third quarter, the two defenses held firm. Although New England outplayed Carolina, neither team was able to find the end zone, which resulted in yet another scoreless quarter. But on the second play of the fourth quarter, Patriots running back Antowain Smith capped a long drive with a touchdown to put New England up 21–10.

Then, something happened that no one expected: the Patriots were punched out. All of that bone-crushing hitting had tired out their defense. The Patriots were out of gas.

What followed next was one of the most entertaining twelve minutes of football in Super Bowl history. Down 21–10 with 14:49 left, the Panthers took off. Delhomme targeted Smith on nearly every passing play, and found him twice on big gains of 18 and 22 yards. Then, DeShaun Foster, the dangerous Carolina back whom the Patriots had locked up all day, snuck around the left end and ran through the exhausted Patriots defense for a 33-yard touchdown.

It was now 21–16. The Panthers failed on a 2-point conversion attempt that could have brought them within a field goal of tying.

Brady immediately drove the Patriots back down-field. It appeared they were about to answer with a score of their own, but a Brady pass was intercepted on the 2-yard line by cornerback Reggie Howard.

On the Panthers' own 15, Delhomme dropped back to pass and uncorked the longest throw of the game—right into the hands of Muhammad, who broke past the Patriots' defense for an 85-yard touchdown, and just like that, Carolina had the lead.

A game that had once been so hard-hitting and low-scoring had turned into an offensive circus. Brady, now desperate with his team down 22–21, found his reliable weapons, wide receiver Troy Brown and running back Kevin Faulk. The Patriots marched downfield on a Carolina defense that was now tired, too. In goal-line situations, Belichick liked to use linebacker Mike Vrabel to provide more blocking on run plays, but Vrabel sometimes snuck past the defense and caught passes. It was a trick play the Patriots had used during the regular season, and on the biggest stage in sports, they tried it once more with the pressure on.

It worked! Brady threw a touchdown to Vrabel and the Patriots had the lead again. After scoring the 2-point conversion, New England led 29–22 with 2:55 left.

But Delhomme would not be outdone. In less than a minute and a half, he marched Carolina back downfield and hit Ricky Proehl with a 12-yard touchdown pass. Proehl had been there before against the Patriots. Two years earlier, when he played for the Rams in Super Bowl XXXVI, he caught the game-tying pass before a Brady-led drive set up Adam Vinatieri's game-winning field goal.

Could Brady do it again? There was 1:13 left. John Kasay, the Carolina kicker, made a huge mistake to help Brady by booting the kickoff out of bounds, giving the Patriots the ball on the 40-yard line.

From there Brady hit Troy Brown for 13 yards.

He then hit Brown again for 13 more.

Forty-four seconds left, and it was happening all over again.

He hit tight end Daniel Graham for 4 and then Deion Branch, who already had ten catches, for 17 yards and the ball was on the Carolina 23 with only seconds left to play.

Out came Vinatieri, just as he'd done two years earlier, to attempt a Super Bowl–winning kick.

In 2002, the winning kick was from 48 yards out. This one was from 41.

The result was the same: Down the middle. Good! The Patriots led 32–29 with four seconds left.

There would be no miracle finish for the Panthers.

The Patriots had won their second Super Bowl in three years. The next year, they would win a third, beating Philadelphia 24–21, solidifying Brady not only as one of the era's great quarterbacks, but perhaps one of the greatest of all time. The same was true of Belichick, the grumpy, unfriendly man who emerged as one of the sharpest coaching minds in football. The Patriots, now winners of three Super Bowls in four years, transformed from a mediocre team into a dynasty in the same category as the great teams of the past. There was, however, no looking back for Brady. In many ways, he and his team were just getting started.

SUPER BOWL XXXVIII
TOP TEN LIST

Nobody wins the Super Bowl every year, but the definition of a dynasty is a premiere team that wins its division year after year and is always in the running for a championship for a long period of time. It's THE team that every other team has its eyes on each season: the one to beat. It's the type of team that every other team in the league fears. Here are ten of the greatest dynasties the league has ever known.

1. San Francisco 49ers (1981–1998): Won five Super Bowls in five matchups. Recorded sixteen seasons with at least 10 wins in an eighteen-year span.
2. Green Bay Packers (1960–1967): Won three NFL titles and two Super Bowls. The championship trophy was eventually named after Green Bay's great coach, Vince Lombardi.
3. Dallas Cowboys (1966–1982): Won two Super Bowls. Made the playoffs in sixteen of seventeen seasons.

An iconic team that boosted the NFL's popularity.

4. Pittsburgh Steelers (1972–1979): The first team to win four Super Bowls, earning victories in all four appearances.

5. New England Patriots (2001–present): Have won four Super Bowls thus far. Went 16-0 in the regular season in 2007. Recorded twelve straight seasons with at least ten wins.

6. Dallas Cowboys (1991–1996): Won three Super Bowls in five years. Brought great football back to Dallas after years of disappointing teams.

7. Oakland / Los Angeles Raiders (1967–1983): Won three Super Bowls in four appearances. Went to seven AFC title games.

8. Miami Dolphins (1970–1985): Two Super Bowl wins in five appearances. Made the playoffs in twelve of sixteen seasons. Recorded the only unbeaten season in NFL history.

9. Denver Broncos (1986–1998): Two Super Bowl wins in five appearances. Made the playoffs in eight of thirteen seasons. The Elway years.

10. Indianapolis Colts (1999–2010): One Super Bowl win in two appearances. Won at least ten games in eleven of twelve seasons.

FOURTH DOWN

SUPER BOWL XLII
A GIANT UPSET

New York Giants vs.
New England Patriots

For decades, Boston and New York have served as battlegrounds for rivalries across all the major sports. There is no greater feud in American sports than the Yankees–Red Sox rivalry. This sense of fierce competition between the two cities even predates professional sports, going all the way back to the Revolutionary War, when Boston and New York competed to become the economic center of the newly formed nation. But sports have served to intensify the rivalry to new heights. The longstanding fight between the Red Sox and Yankees has fueled mutual hatred among players and fans on both sides.

The same is true for the Celtics and Knicks, as well as the Bruins and Rangers.

The Patriots–Jets rivalry has been the major Boston–New York slugfest in the NFL. The divisional foes have faced off when both teams were at their best. They've also had a habit of either stealing each other's players or going after the same free agents.

The Patriots and the Giants had never exactly been rivals. They shared no special history or bad blood. They had never met in the Super Bowl and they only played each other every four years. The Giants, weirdly, even had a lot of old fans in New England, because before the AFL was founded in 1960, they were the closest pro football team to Boston.

In the 2007 season, however, that all changed. After putting on one of the greatest Super Bowls of all time, a rivalry between the Patriots and Giants was instantly born.

It all started the year before, in the AFC Championship Game between the Patriots and the Colts. About halfway through the game, the Patriots led 21–3 and appeared to be headed to their fourth Super Bowl in six years. The success of the 2006 Patriots was surprising, because they weren't as great a team as they'd been in

2004. The current squad was weak defensively, especially in the middle of the field, and its wide receivers were substandard. Still, up 18 points, it appeared they were good enough to get to the Super Bowl.

Then the Colts woke up. All of a sudden, the Patriots' weaknesses on both offense and defense were exposed. Peyton Manning led a furious charge against his greatest rivals and beat the Patriots in a 38–34 thriller. The Colts advanced to the Super Bowl, and Manning won his first (and only) Lombardi Trophy over Chicago.

Talk about dominoes! It was bad enough to blow a lead that would have put them in the Super Bowl, but to lose to Manning and then see him win it all was too much for New England to handle.

So, the Patriots did something they never did: They went out and spent enough cash to form the best team money could buy. They signed Randy Moss, one of the greatest wide receivers of all time. Many people think Moss was the second-best receiver ever to play, behind the great Jerry Rice of San Francisco. Moss was tall and fast and had great hands. He was the kind of offensive weapon that Tom Brady had never had the opportunity to play alongside.

To make sure defenses didn't focus solely on Moss,

the Patriots also acquired Wes Welker, a shifty possession receiver who was tough and fearless. If Welker and Moss weren't enough, the Patriots then signed another lightning-fast pass-catcher, Donté Stallworth.

It was a way to address a dirty little secret that had bothered Patriots fans and Brady for years: As talented a quarterback as Tom Brady was, unlike the other all-time greats, he never had a top wide receiver to target. Brady's childhood idol, Joe Montana, had Jerry Rice. Terry Bradshaw had Lynn Swann. Troy Aikman had Michael Irvin.

Now that Brady had Moss, why, the Patriots might not lose a single game . . .

. . . and after the first eight weeks of the season, they were undefeated.

If that wasn't impressive enough, they had scored at least 34 points in every game! The offense was unstoppable. If the defense focused on Moss, Brady would throw to Welker. If they focused on Welker, Moss might be open deep. If they shut down Welker and Moss, Brady would throw to Stallworth or running back Kevin Faulk or Jabar Gaffney, the fourth wide receiver.

When they beat Washington 52–7 to go 8-0, the

talk started: Maybe this would be the first team since the 1972 Dolphins to go unbeaten. The next week, they slipped by Peyton Manning and the Colts, 24–20, despite scoring their lowest total of the season. But in their next matchup, they poured on the points, crushing Buffalo 56–10, the second time they'd scored 50 points in the season.

The pressure mounted, but the Patriots kept winning, beating Philadelphia and Pittsburgh and escaping Baltimore 27–24, in a game they probably should have lost.

On the last day of the season, they went to New York to play the Giants. In a hard-fought game, the Patriots trailed 21–16 at the half. The Giants, led by Peyton Manning's little brother Eli at quarterback, gave the Patriots all they could handle. The Giants led 28–16 before Moss caught a 65-yard touchdown pass from Brady. A few drives later, the Patriots finally regained a lead. The Patriots held on to win 38–35, but the Giants knew they could play with the first team in NFL history to go unbeaten in a sixteen-game regular season. The Dolphins went 14-0 before the season was extended. The Patriots' off-season spending spree had clearly paid off.

The playoffs were a struggle because of the pressure of winning and remaining undefeated, but the Patriots kept on track, beating Jacksonville 31–20 and then San Diego 21–12 in the AFC title game. They had reached the Super Bowl. The Patriots were 18-0, and one more game remained. One last game to achieve complete perfection.

The only team that really gave them problems in the NFC was the Giants, but the Giants were a long shot to even make it to the Super Bowl. After a 6-2 start, they'd struggled in the second half of the regular season, finishing 10-6, squeaking into the playoffs by earning a wild card spot. In fact, the Giants had played so unevenly there was a rumor that Tom Coughlin, the Giants coach, would be fired at the end of the season.

But New York went on the road, first to Tampa Bay, where they beat the Buccaneers 24–14. Then they went to play against division rival Dallas, and upset the favored Cowboys 21–17. And once more, they went on the road to Green Bay, "Title Town", to play the Packers in the NFC title game.

The Packers were clear favorites. They were at home, and the weather was freezing. Green Bay loved to play in the cold, mostly because their opponents weren't used to the frigid conditions.

No matter—the Giants won again—this time in overtime.

That meant that the Patriots would play the Giants, the team that had nearly shattered their perfection in the final week of the regular season, for the chance to go undefeated, a perfect 19-0.

The Giants were unafraid. In fact, they were so confident, Michael Strahan, the Hall of Fame defensive end, predicted the high-scoring Patriots wouldn't even score 20 points.

From the start, something was different about this game. The Giants' defensive front line dominated the game. Brady couldn't find any space to throw. He also seemed to be moving poorly on an injured leg. Strahan and fellow defensive ends Osi Umenyiora and Justin Tuck were all over him. The Patriots couldn't run the ball either against New York's line. The game was not the lights-out, high-scoring affair people predicted it would be.

At halftime, the Patriots led 7–3. 7–3? This was the team that had scored 30 points in thirteen out of eighteen games!

Neither team scored in the third quarter. The game was being played exactly the way the Giants were hoping it would go down.

On their first drive of the fourth quarter, the Giants came out firing. Manning hurled a 45-yard pass to his tight end Kevin Boss. Then, with eleven minutes left, the Giants scored their first touchdown of the game on a 5-yard pass to David Tyree, his first of the season. The Giants led 10–7 with eleven minutes to go.

Could this be happening? The Patriots were favored by 12.5 points to win, but they still hadn't cracked double digits!

Brady got the ball back with 7:54 left, on his 20-yard line, down 10–7.

These are the championship moments, and Brady was the guy you wanted out on the field with the season on the line.

He wasted no time. On the first play, Brady hit Welker for 5 yards and then Moss for 10. Laurence Maroney, the running back, ran for 9 more. Then, like a machine, Brady completed passes to Welker, Faulk, Welker, Moss, and Welker again. Suddenly the Patriots were at the Giants' 6-yard line with 2:49 to go.

If Brady felt the pressure of the big stage, he didn't

show it. Two plays later, he hit Moss for the go-ahead touchdown. The Patriots led 14–10 with 2:42 left.

Two minutes and forty-two seconds away from an undefeated season.

Manning took the ball from the Giants' 17-yard line, 83 yards away from victory. It was touchdown or bust; a field goal wouldn't cut it. The Patriots' defense needed to keep the Giants out of the end zone.

On the Giants' sideline, Strahan encouraged his team. "Seventeen–fourteen! Seventeen–fourteen! That's the final score," he said to his teammates. "One touchdown and we're world champions. If you believe it, it will happen!"

Manning immediately moved the ball, finding the Giants' all-time leading receiver, Amani Toomer, twice. The second catch came on third and 10, but was good for only 9 yards. The Giants were forced to go for it on fourth down with the season on the line. On fourth and 1, the bruising running back Brandon Jacobs plowed forward with a 2-yard run. The Giants were still alive.

With 1:20 left on the clock, the Giants near midfield, Manning dropped back and threw a long pass intended for David Tyree, but the ball sailed right toward Patriots cornerback Asante Samuel for what looked like a sure interception. The Giants were finished. The undefeated season was going to happen . . .

Until the ball bounced off Samuel's hand, incomplete.

On third and 5, Manning was caught by Patriots defensive end Adalius Thomas. Thomas held his jersey, but Manning scrambled free to his right and threw a desperation pass down the middle of the field to Tyree.

The ball floated in the air. Fans across the country held their breath.

Tyree jumped and grabbed the ball with one hand, but New England safety Rodney Harrison had him covered, so Tyree lodged the ball between his right hand and his helmet! He had caught the ball with his helmet!

It was one of the greatest catches, if not *the* greatest catch, in Super Bowl history.

Fifty-nine seconds left. Following the remarkable 32-yard gain, the ball was on the New England 24.

Manning found wide receiver Steve Smith (not the same Steve Smith who played for Carolina) on the right sideline for 12 more yards.

Forty-five seconds left.

First down. Manning dropped back, looked to his left for Burress, who was wide open in the end zone.

The ball went up in the air. Burress came down with it. Touchdown!

Strahan's predictions came true: The Giants held the Patriots to under 20 points, and the final score was 17–14 Giants. The Patriots' season-long dominance of the entire league ended on the final drive of the season, when a guy caught a ball with his helmet and the Giants, who'd barely made the playoffs, pulled off one of the greatest upsets in Super Bowl history. Eli Manning, long overshadowed by his big brother Peyton, proved that he could hang with—and beat—the best the league had to offer. Not only that, but he sealed his reputation as the guy you wanted on the field with the game on the line in the fourth quarter. When all was said and done, one sideline experienced a sense of bitter defeat. On the other, players were filled with the best feeling in the world. Improbably, David had taken down Goliath. The Giants were champions.

SUPER BOWL XLII
TOP TEN LIST

espite a 16-0 regular season record, the Patriots didn't end the year undefeated, leaving the 1972 Dolphins as the only team in the Super Bowl era to achieve perfection. The Giants shocked the world by stepping onto the big stage and beating Tom Brady and the Patriots when it counted the most. But they weren't the only team that overcame long odds in a do-or-die game: here are the top ten most memorable upsets in playoff history.

1. Super Bowl III, New York Jets vs. Baltimore Colts: After boldly guaranteeing victory, Joe Namath makes good on his promise and the Jets become the first AFL team to win the Big Game.
2. Super Bowl XXVI, New England Patriots vs. St. Louis Rams: The Patriots dynasty is born as Tom Brady outduels Kurt Warner and the "Greatest

Show on Turf" offense to win the franchise's first championship.

3. 1996 AFC divisional playoffs, Jacksonville Jaguars vs. Denver Broncos: The Jaguars, in only their second year of existence, enter the game as 14.5-point underdogs, but overcome Elway and the 13-3 Broncos. The Jaguars' head coach that year? Tom Coughlin, better known these days for coaching the New York Giants to a couple of Super Bowl wins.

4. 1998 NFC championship, Minnesota Vikings vs. Atlanta Falcons: Minnesota goes 15-1 in the regular season, looking all but invincible, but fails to reach the Super Bowl as Atlanta pulls off the upset, 30–27.

5. 1987 NFC divisional playoffs, San Francisco 49ers vs. Minnesota Vikings: Vikings wide receiver Anthony Carter has the game of his life, catching 10 passes for 227 yards, helping to defeat the top-seeded 49ers.

6. 1995 AFC championship, San Diego Chargers vs. Pittsburgh Steelers: Playing in the cold of Pittsburgh, the Steelers are heavily favored,

but San Diego finishes the game by scoring 14
unanswered points on their way to winning
by 4, advancing to their first Super Bowl in
franchise history. (They would lose to the mighty
49ers.)

7. 1986 AFC championship, New England Patriots
    vs. Miami Dolphins: The Patriots' running game
    steals the show from Dolphins quarterback
    Dan Marino, racking up 255 rushing yards in a
    surprisingly lopsided 31–14 victory, depriving
    the world of the expected Miami–Chicago Super
    Bowl showdown. New England goes on to get
    mauled by the Bears.

8. Super Bowl XLII, New England Patriots vs. New
    York Giants: Giants wide receiver David Tyree
    makes his incredible "Helmet Catch." Just a few
    plays later, Eli Manning connects with Plaxico
    Burress for the touchdown that crushes the
    Patriots' hopes of a 19-0 unbeaten season.

9. Super Bowl XLVI, New England Patriots vs. New
    York Giants: In a rematch, aided by yet another
    miracle last-minute catch (this one by Mario
    Manningham), the Giants deny the Patriots a

chance for revenge, winning the championship despite a mediocre 9-7 regular season record.

10. 1979 NFC divisional playoffs: Dallas Cowboys vs. St. Louis Rams: After losing to the Cowboys 30–6 in the regular season, the Rams narrowly defeat the top-seeded Cowboys 21–19, on their way to becoming the first team to reach the Super Bowl with fewer than ten wins.

SUPER BOWL XLIII WINNING AND LOSING—BY A HAIR

PITTSBURGH STEELERS VS. ARIZONA CARDINALS

The first forty-five minutes of Super Bowl XLIII were a throwback to the awful old days when a legendary franchise played against a Cinderella team and the results were predictable: The clock struck twelve on Cinderella, but not before an epic beatdown occurred. In the old days, Cinderella never had a chance.

In 2009, it seemed as though nothing had changed. At Raymond James Stadium in Tampa, the mighty Pittsburgh Steelers, who had reached the Super Bowl six times and won five of them over their storied history, had the lead against the untested Arizona Cardinals. Not only had the Cardinals never won the Super Bowl, they had never even *been* to the Super Bowl or reached the conference championship game before. The Cardinals had been so bad historically that they hadn't played for a championship since 1948, back when they were known as the Chicago Cardinals.

Following twelve seasons in Chicago, the Cardinals moved to St. Louis in 1960, where they played until 1987. In 1988, they moved to Phoenix and became the Phoenix Cardinals. In 1994, they stayed in town but changed their name once again to the Arizona Cardinals. Though they'd changed their name and location over the years, one aspect of the team remained the same: they always struggled to succeed.

Finally, after that long journey, after years of disappointment, here they were in the Super Bowl playing against one of the greatest franchises in NFL history, a team that had been around since 1933, never changed their name, and barely ever changed their uniforms or owners. They were the Steelers, the team that seemed to always be in the hunt.

The Steelers were cruising along for most of the game. On their first two drives, they put points on the board, and took an early lead. By the third quarter, with Pittsburgh leading 20–7, the game began to feel like one of those old boring Super Bowls from the 1980s, when one team seemed happy just to have an opportunity to play in the Big Game, but the other team dominated from the start.

Even the Cardinals' best moment of the first half—mounting an impressive drive toward the end of the half that nearly gave them the lead—got upstaged by the Steelers. Kurt Warner, the great quarterback who'd taken the Rams to the Super Bowl twice, was now the Cardinals quarterback. He dropped back to pass and threw into the end zone, where his pass was intercepted by Steelers linebacker James Harrison. With only a few seconds remaining in the half, the expected move was for Harrison to kneel, let time expire, and be happy with the Steelers' lead.

Except, the interception didn't end the half. Harrison, despite his huge size, was very athletic. He took Warner's pass out of the air and then took off! Down the sideline he went, and it looked like nearly the entire Cardinals team had a shot to get him. All they had to do was knock Harrison out of bounds because there was no time left on the clock.

But they couldn't bring him down! Harrison jumped over one guy and knocked over another. He raced *100* yards and scored an improbable touchdown, easily the greatest interception return for a touchdown in Super Bowl history. That gave the Steelers a 17–7 lead at halftime and, once again, the Cardinals looked done.

It was sort of fitting, anyway. The Cardinals weren't a great team. They had won only nine games all season, just barely staying above a .500 winning percentage. A nine-win playoff team didn't command much respect in the first place.

In the playoffs, though, the Cardinals proved to be tough. They beat Atlanta, destroyed Carolina on the road, and then, in their first-ever NFC title game, defeated a skilled Philadelphia team 32–25 to reach the Super Bowl. Undeterred by the odds, Arizona had one more team to beat to win big.

The Steelers were a different story—bursting with talent, it was no surprise that they'd made it all the way to the Super Bowl. That was especially true considering every team in the league got a lucky break when Tom Brady, the Patriots quarterback, tore ligaments in his knee after taking a shattering hit in the first game of the season. Every team except New England, of course. The Patriots, the team that had gone undefeated a year earlier before losing a classic Super Bowl to the Giants, were forced to play without their fearless leader. The Patriots found a way to win eleven games, but didn't make the playoffs.

With Tom Brady absent, the Steelers took advantage, beating their archrival Baltimore in a black-and-blue AFC Championship Game where both teams hit each other so hard, it was a miracle no one was seriously injured.

Now they were just thirty minutes away from winning their second Super Bowl in five years. Led by Ben Roethlisberger, their strong, sturdy quarterback who constantly refused to go down under pressure, Pittsburgh had beaten Seattle three years prior to win Super Bowl XL. Roethlisberger was downright tenacious, and he had the sort of giant build that made it nearly impossible to bring him down, earning him the nickname "Big Ben." A fearless leader on the field, Roethlisberger had a knack for making timely plays in dire circumstances.

After an almost boring third quarter, with only a Pittsburgh field goal to show for it, the Steelers appeared to be coasting their way to yet another championship when, all of a sudden, things went haywire.

The Cardinals, after sleepwalking all game, woke up and came out firing. Warner found his great weapon, Larry Fitzgerald, all over the field. Playing in a no-huddle offense, the pair started an eight-play drive that ended in a Warner-to-Fitzgerald touchdown on a leaping fade route, and suddenly it was 20–14 with 7:41 left. The drive took just under four minutes and kept Arizona's hope alive.

What had once been a sure victory for Pittsburgh turned into a battle between two teams and two quarterbacks who were known for rising to the occasion.

After two uneventful drives, the Cardinals were forced to punt the ball back to Pittsburgh with under four minutes left in the game. Punter Ben Graham came out and executed a perfect punt, pinning the Steelers at their own 1-yard line. On third and 10, in trouble and forced to throw from inside his own end zone, Roethlisberger found speedy receiver Santonio Holmes for 19 yards.

But right when Pittsburgh thought they'd earned some breathing room, center Justin Hartwig was flagged for holding. *In the end zone.* By rule, that meant a safety: 2 more points for Arizona, and the ball back on the next possession!

Now, with 3:04 left, it was 20–16, Pittsburgh, and the Cardinals weren't done yet.

After struggling to score all game, it took less than twenty seconds for Warner to drop back on second and 10 from his 36 and hit Fitzgerald up the middle for what should have been a short gain, but Fitzgerald broke free from everyone and raced 64 yards for a touchdown. The Cardinals now led 23–20!

How could this be happening? In a flash, the game transformed from a ho-hum Super Bowl win for Pittsburgh into a desperate situation. The Cardinals, who hadn't won a championship in over sixty years, were on the verge of finishing off one of the great NFL franchises.

Big Ben Roethlisberger was unfazed. Throughout his career, he'd made a habit of staying on his feet no matter the pressure thrown his way. He went right to work from his 22, and completed three passes for more than 10 yards each, two to Holmes and one to Nate Washington. Then, Roethlisberger picked up four more yards on a quarterback scramble to get the ball into Arizona territory with 1:02 left.

Time-out, Pittsburgh.

Big Ben dropped back once more. The rush came, but Roethlisberger, fearless as ever, kept his eyes downfield. He hit a streaking Holmes again, this time for 40 yards, moving the ball to the 6-yard line as the clock ran down.

Forty-nine seconds left. Time-out, Pittsburgh.

Down by 3. Second down and goal. A short field goal would tie the game, but Pittsburgh coach Mike Tomlin and Roethlisberger weren't interested in giving Arizona another chance to score.

Time to go for the win.

Big Ben dropped back, looking left, looking right. At the last second, he looked again to his right and threw to the far corner of the end zone. There was Holmes, stretched out, on his tiptoes. With his feet mere inches away from the sideline, the ball landed in his hands, and incredibly, he managed to stay inbounds.

Touchdown, Steelers. They now led 27–23!

For so long, the Steelers were known for their defense. The famous Steel Curtain made them legends in the 1970s, and now the defense needed to hold for thirty-nine seconds and the Steelers would be champions once more.

No problem. Warner was sacked, he fumbled, and Pittsburgh recovered the ball.

The Cardinals had come *so* close with that furious rally, but the Roethlisberger-led Steelers, already having proved themselves once in the high-pressure environment of the Super Bowl, prevailed in the end. Yet in turning a lackluster competition into a wild nail-biter of a football game, Arizona had shown they belonged in the championship fight. Unfortunately for them, their comeback came up short.

Roethlisberger had won his second Super Bowl title. Tomlin, only the third African American to coach in a Super Bowl and the second to win, won his first, becoming the youngest head coach in Super Bowl history to accomplish the feat. The Steelers as a team also made history: They became the first team to win six Super Bowl championships. The NFL had certainly changed since the days when a few elite franchises dominated and newcomers didn't stand a chance. But sometimes, the old ways still held.

SUPER BOWL XLIII
TOP TEN LIST

James Harrison's 100-yard dash might be the greatest defensive play in the history of the Super Bowl. Though it might be the greatest, it certainly wasn't the first incredible defensive moment in a Super Bowl. Here are the ten greatest defensive feats in Super Bowl history.

1. James Harrison (Pittsburgh Steelers, linebacker), Super Bowl XLIV: With no time left in the first half, Harrison intercepts Kurt Warner on the goal line and runs the ball back 100 yards, past all eleven guys, and scores!

2. Chuck Howley (Dallas Cowboys, linebacker), Super Bowl V: Two interceptions and a fumble recovery. To this day, Howley is the only Super Bowl MVP to play on the losing team!

3. Tracy Porter (New Orleans Saints, cornerback), Super Bowl XLIV: Intercepts Peyton Manning at

the Saints' 26-yard line in the final moments of the game and runs the ball back 74 yards for the score that seals the Super Bowl for New Orleans over Indianapolis.

4. Dan Bunz (San Francisco 49ers, linebacker), Super Bowl XVI: Third-down-and-goal from the 1-yard line. Running back Charles Alexander catches a pass from quarterback Ken Anderson and turns to score. Bunz flies toward Alexander, grabs him by the waist, and hurls him to the ground shy of the end zone. The 49ers hold off the Bengals to win the Super Bowl.

5. Malcolm Butler (New England Patriots, cornerback), Super Bowl XLIX: With the clock winding down and the Seahawks about to score the winning touchdown, Butler steps in front of receiver Ricardo Lockette and intercepts a Russell Wilson pass on the goal line. The Patriots win the Super Bowl.

6. Mike Jones (St. Louis Rams, linebacker), Super Bowl XXXIV: As time expires, Jones saves the day for the Rams with a goal-line tackle of Tennessee Titans receiver Kevin Dyson. Rams win by a touchdown.

7. 2013 Baltimore Ravens, Super Bowl XLVII: A huge goal-line stand stops San Francisco in the final minutes of the game. Ravens win 34–31.

8. 1985 Bears, Super Bowl XX: The Bears' ferocious defense holds New England to *seven* rushing yards total on the way to a 36-point victory.

9. Willie Brown (Oakland Raiders, cornerback), Super Bowl XI: Brown's fourth-quarter 75-yard interception return for a touchdown seals the win against the Vikings.

10. L. C. Greenwood (Pittsburgh Steelers, defensive end), Super Bowl X: Sacks the great Roger Staubach four times as the Steel Curtain shuts down the Cowboys' offense.

SUPER BOWL XLIV SCORE ONE FOR THE UNDERDOGS

~~~~~~

NEW ORLEANS SAINTS VS. INDIANAPOLIS COLTS

For the fans, sports are first and foremost supposed to be about fun, about feeling good. In today's media-crazed world, business often gets in the way, and the excitement of the game can be overshadowed by talk of enormous contracts and the bad decisions some players make off the field. For better or worse, sports have become more than just a game and a source of entertainment.

Sometimes, though, the way that sports transcend entertainment can mean the world to fans. When life is hard, sports can be the one thing that makes people forget their problems. It can be the one place where their struggles no longer matter, just for a little while, and the most important thing in the world can be something as simple as a touchdown or the defense making a goal-line stand. Sports can be so much more than a game—they can serve as a refuge from the worries of life and a ray of hope in difficult times.

Such was the case in New Orleans in 2005, when the city suffered through Hurricane Katrina, one of the worst disasters in American history. Due to the storm and the flooding it caused, nearly two thousand people died, and many more were injured, while others lost their homes and livelihoods.

In the face of that kind of devastation, where the entire city of New Orleans was under an extended state of emergency, sports didn't seem to matter that much. When Katrina hit in August of 2005, the Louisiana Superdome, the home of the city's football team, the Saints, served as a homeless shelter for the people who lost their homes due to the flooding. Some New Orleans residents were moved to shelters in Houston. Still others left town to live with family in nearby places like Mobile, Alabama, and Texas.

Slowly, painfully, the people of New Orleans began to put the pieces of their lives together. As they did, the Saints were there to help provide a source of happiness and serve as a rallying point for fans.

Sometimes, in sad situations, you have to find some humor. It keeps you going. In the case of the New Orleans Saints, the joke was that they were one of those historically bad teams that not only had never won a championship, they were so bad that people used to laugh at just how abysmal they were. For example:

1. New Orleans fans used to come to the stadium wearing bags on their heads, because the Saints were so awful people didn't want to be seen at their games.
2. The Saints' lackluster performances earned them the unfortunate nickname "The Ain'ts."

In a lot of ways, New Orleans was like the Patriots, a team that had always been terrible in the twentieth century, but became an elite team in the twenty-first. The transformation was due in part to good management, who recruited top talent, and made sure to hold on to that talent by paying their players well.

In the twenty-first century, the NFL is a quarterback's game, and the first step to the Saints becoming great was acquiring Drew Brees from the San Diego Chargers. Brees was an offensive genius. He wasn't a big guy, just about six feet tall (considered short for a quarterback), but boy, could Drew Brees read a defense. His mind was like a computer. He could see the field so well, he always spotted the open receiver.

Even in the twenty-first century, though, it takes more than a quarterback to excel. A quarterback needs targets, so the Saints found great players for Brees to throw to. Tight end Jeremy Shockey came from the Giants, and he had already won a Super Bowl. He was a former Rookie of the Year who could run routes as well as he could block. There was a trio of big, speedy receivers in Marques Colston, Devery Henderson, and Robert Meachem. An electric pair of running backs who could run and catch the ball, Pierre Thomas and Reggie Bush, rounded out the offense. Bush had won the Heisman Trophy when he played at the University of Southern California.

The Saints were loaded offensively, and in addition to their skilled cast of players, they had one other advantage: They played indoors at the Superdome.

Playing indoors, without wind, heat, cold, or rain, provided excellent playing conditions. It also meant no slippery footballs, no windy afternoons, and it aided the Saints in becoming an offensive machine.

In 2009, with all the pieces assembled, the Saints started off with a bang. In Week 1, they put up 45 points against the Lions at home and then went to Philadelphia the next week and scored 48 more. As the season went on, they continued to pile on the points, their dangerous offense plowing through defenses week after week. New Orleans's biggest test of the season came in Week 12, in a Monday-night showdown at home against the Patriots. Spectators around the country thought they were watching a Super Bowl preview. The promise of a hard-fought standoff never came to fruition, though. Instead, the game turned into a classic display of Brees and Colston. Brees threw for five touchdowns and Colston totaled 121 yards receiving. The final score was 38–17, Saints.

The Saints' record was now 11-0 . . .

The rejuvenated Saints were no longer the butt of jokes. Now, a different story took hold: they were the team that was winning for the city of New Orleans, playing for a broken place they cared for deeply and for all the people who'd lost loved ones because of Hurricane Katrina.

The next two weeks, they beat Washington in overtime and narrowly escaped the Falcons to go 13-0. Was it really possible that the Saints, just three years after the Patriots went 16-0, could go undefeated? And if one team with a chance to go unbeaten wasn't enough to get fans excited, in the AFC, the Indianapolis Colts were also undefeated at 13-0! Could *two* teams go undefeated in the same season for the first time in NFL history? It was the makings of a dream Super Bowl matchup.

When the Super Bowl kicked off in Miami on Sunday, February 7, 2010, neither team participating was undefeated, but it was still the Colts and the Saints who faced off. The Colts had gone 14-0 before deciding to rest their best players to keep them from getting hurt, and lost their last two games of the season. The Saints, meanwhile, had lost their last three games of the year and finished the regular season with a record of 13-3. Still, both swept through the playoffs and found their way to the Super Bowl, the Saints playing for a devastated city, and the Colts trying to win their second championship in four years. There was a lot on the line for both sides: A win for New Orleans would bring joy to a city that had known too much sadness for the past few years. For Peyton Manning, the great Colts quarterback, a win would secure his legacy.

Manning was so good, virtually everyone in football believed him to be the best quarterback in the game. He threw for the most touchdowns seemingly every year. His teams could move the ball downfield almost at will. The way he commanded his offense at the line of scrimmage suggested he understood everything one could possibly know about quarterbacking. His was the most famous face in the league.

Yet, in past playoffs, he'd often come up short. His postseason record caused many fans and analysts to rank him below his greatest rival, Patriots quarterback Tom Brady. The question of who was better had endured over the years. Manning was flashier, with better statistics, but Brady won more. The Patriots won most of their head-to-head meetings against the Colts. Brady had three Super Bowl rings; Manning had one. Another Super Bowl win for Manning would help him get closer to evening the score.

Two of the great offensive teams put on a dazzling

offensive show in the Super Bowl. Manning and Brees threw a combined 84 passing attempts, but it took some time for the Saints to get going, and they could only muster 6 points in the first half. The Colts, on the other hand, found early success, scoring on their first two drives. At halftime they led 10–6.

After a relatively low-scoring first half, the third quarter began with an unexpected gamble by New Orleans. The Saints came out and immediately attempted an onside kick, the first team to do so before the fourth quarter in a playoff game. The unexpected, bold move paid off. New Orleans recovered the ball near midfield. From there, Brees got hot to start the second half. He moved the ball into the red zone, and on first and 10 from Indianapolis's 16-yard line, he stepped back quickly, scanning left to right, and threw a touchdown pass to Thomas to give the Saints their first lead.

Their lead was short-lived, though. Manning came right back, orchestrating a 76-yard drive that was capped off by a 4-yard rushing touchdown by running back Joseph Addai. The Colts now led 17–13.

New Orleans managed to inch closer to the Colts by hitting a field goal, but Indianapolis maintained a 17–16 lead to start the final quarter. Manning was fifteen minutes away from winning his second Super Bowl, and Brees needed a comeback as Saints fans looked on with bated breath. So many people in New Orleans believed that after the hurricane and the flood the Saints were *supposed* to win the Super Bowl. The city was in dire need of a reason to celebrate.

With 10:39 left in the game, down by one, Brees went into action, using all of his marvelous weapons. Bush ran for 12 yards, darting in and away from defenders, showing off his superior moves. Then Thomas caught a pass for 5, and Henderson reeled in another for 6. Brees was getting all of his teammates involved. Bush, Colston, Meachem, and David Thomas all caught passes as the Saints drove downfield.

From the Indianapolis 2-yard line, with 5:46 left, Brees hit Shockey for the go-ahead touchdown. The city of New Orleans went crazy, and crazier still when the successful 2-point attempt gave them a 24–17 lead.

It wasn't over yet, though. Peyton Manning, one of the greatest of all time, had the ball, with a lot of game left.

Manning did the same thing Brees did, dropping back, watching for any hole in the New Orleans defense.

He had his own group of dangerous weapons, and he found them as Indianapolis charged toward the tying score. Manning found wide receivers Pierre Garcon and Reggie Wayne as the Colts advanced to the New Orleans 31-yard line with 3:29 left. A touchdown felt all but inevitable when Manning was on a roll like this.

Third down and 5: Manning stepped back, looked downfield, and threw short to his left. He didn't see cornerback Tracy Porter barreling toward the ball until it was too late. Porter intercepted the ball and ran 69 yards in the other direction for a touchdown.

The Saints led 31–17, and there would be no comeback from Manning. After more than forty years of waiting, the Saints were finally Super Bowl champions. The win could not have come at a more welcome moment in New Orleans's history. After four years of devastation and sadness, the city of New Orleans finally had something to cheer about. For the span of a football game and a celebration, the city could forget its struggles, consumed by the pure joy of victory. There would be other Super Bowl wins for other teams, but few of them, if any, meant more to a city than the Saints' victory did to New Orleans in 2010.

SUPER BOWL XLIV
TOP TEN LIST

Some franchises seem to win year after year, always in the hunt for the playoffs. But other teams, like the New Orleans Saints, have only recently found their way to becoming winners after years and years of losing. The 2009 Saints started a new chapter in their team's history. Here are ten teams who were once known for losing, and suddenly transformed into winners.

1. 2009 New Orleans Saints: The Saints didn't play in their first playoff game until 1987, and had *never* played in an NFC championship before 2009—the year they won the Super Bowl.

2. 2008 Arizona Cardinals: The Cardinals had not played for a championship since 1948, back when they were the Chicago Cardinals. This was the year they would make it all the way to their first

Super Bowl, only to be defeated by the Steelers in a nail-biter.

3. 1996 New England Patriots: From 1989 to 1993, the Patriots lost sixty-one of eighty games before turning things around and reaching the Super Bowl under legendary head coach Bill Parcells. They would then lose to Brett Favre and the Packers in Super Bowl XXXI.

4. 1981 Cincinnati Bengals: The Bengals went 4-12 in 1978, 4-12 in 1979, 6-10 in 1980, and made the Super Bowl in 1981.

5. 1981 San Francisco 49ers: The 49ers were best known for having good seasons, only to lose to Dallas in the playoffs. Bill Walsh and Joe Montana changed that and created a dynasty.

6. 1979 Tampa Bay Buccaneers: In 1976, the inaugural year of their franchise, the Buccaneers became the first team in the Super Bowl era to lose *all* of their games. Three years later, they reached the NFC title game, losing a close one to the Rams.

7. 2002 Tampa Bay Buccaneers: For two decades, ever since that surprising 1979 season, the Bucs

had been known for one thing: losing. Then, under first-year head coach Jon Gruden, they formed one of the greatest defenses in NFL history and destroyed the Raiders 48–21 in Super Bowl XXXVII.

8. 1966 Dallas Cowboys: The Cowboys had never made the playoffs in their previous six years of existence. From 1966 to 1985, they made the playoffs in eighteen of twenty seasons and won two Super Bowls. 1966 was the start of the run.

9. 1995 Green Bay Packers: Following years of mediocre play in the '70s and '80s, the '95 Packers, led by legendary quarterback Brett Favre, brought winning football back to Green Bay. The Packers would win the Super Bowl the following season.

10. 1992 Dallas Cowboys: After plunging back to earth by going 1-15 three years prior, the Cowboys reached the top again, beating Buffalo 52–17 in Super Bowl XXVII.

SUPER BOWL XLVI
THE REMATCH,
PART II

NEW YORK GIANTS VS.
NEW ENGLAND PATRIOTS

For four years, the New England Patriots had waited for this moment, to be back on the field playing for a championship for the first time since losing to the New York Giants in a game that shattered their hopes of going undefeated.

Those four years were long ones. The next season after the Giants stunned the Patriots in the Super Bowl, Tom Brady tore his knee up in the very first game of the season and missed the rest of the year. There were other disappointments along the way, but the sting of that Super Bowl loss, of being so close to history and not making it, could only be softened by a chance for redemption. Or, perhaps, revenge.

On Sunday, February 5, 2012, the Patriots took the field in the Super Bowl for the first time since their missed opportunity in Arizona four years earlier. As if the stakes weren't high enough, their opponent once again was the New York Giants, the team that had denied them perfection in 2008.

The rematch was supposed to be different. The first loss to the Giants was an upset, and upsets happen, but only so often. The Patriots were determined to avoid a repeat performance. Tom Brady was now known as one of the all-time great quarterbacks, and winning that fourth Super Bowl would put him in a club with just two other members: Terry Bradshaw of the Steelers, and Brady's idol, Joe Montana of the 49ers.

The 2011 Patriots were not expected to be a great team, but they became one, starting off hot at 5-1, before losing two straight to Pittsburgh and, yes, the Giants, at home, 24–20. Again, there was something about the Giants' defense that gave the Patriots problems. Michael Strahan may have retired, yet the Giants were still very good up front, stacked with tough defensive linemen like Jason Pierre-Paul, Osi Umenyiora, and Justin Tuck, who were able to push the Patriots' offensive line backward, crowding Brady, making it difficult for him to throw. There was also something about the Giants' quarterback, Eli Manning, who despite having fairly average seasons statistically was developing a reputation for being clutch, outplaying Brady in their head-to-head matchups. In Week 9, when the Giants had stifled the Patriots' offense and squeaked out yet another close win, the Patriots had led 20–17 with 1:36 left, but Eli Manning orchestrated a remarkably quick 80-yard touchdown drive, and the Giants sealed the deal with fifteen seconds left. The ending felt eerily similar to the conclusion of Super Bowl XLII.

That loss to the Giants must've lit a fire in the Patriots, because they finished the season with eight straight victories, including a big win over rival Indianapolis in which Brady defeated his nemesis Peyton Manning yet again. Where the Patriots cruised through the regular season, the Giants struggled, saving their best football for the playoffs. In the regular season, New York was far from a great team.

The 2011–2012 team was 9-7 on the year, and after beating the Patriots in Week 9, the Giants wound up losing four straight games and five of six. The struggling Giants almost didn't even make the playoffs. The storyline for the mediocre Giants for most of the season was whether or not they would fire their coach, Tom Coughlin, at the end of the year.

If you make the playoffs, though, you have a chance to go all the way, and the Giants snuck in at 9-7. They started the playoffs with a beatdown win against Atlanta in the NFC wild card game. The Giants' defense didn't allow an offensive score all game, ultimately winning 24–2. The next week, New York went to Green Bay, just as they had done during their previous Super Bowl run, and beat the Packers, this time handily, 37–20, setting up an NFC title game against the San Francisco 49ers.

The game was played in San Francisco and in another classic, the 49ers and Giants dueled and hit and crunched each other throughout the afternoon. The 49ers led 14–10 in the fourth quarter until backup wide receiver Kyle Williams fumbled on a punt return. The Giants recovered and later scored the go-ahead touchdown.

The 49ers fought back and scored a game-tying field goal in the middle of the fourth quarter. The game was still tied at the end of regulation. In overtime, both teams failed on their first opportunities. When the Giants punted the ball back to the 49ers, Williams fumbled *again*. The Giants recovered deep in 49ers territory, and four plays later, Lawrence Tynes kicked the game-winner and sent the Giants back to the Super Bowl.

This game was supposed to be different from the 2008 Super Bowl. The Patriots were supposed to be ready for the Giants. This time, they were supposed to dominate. New England was supposed to be better, having won ten straight games since losing to the Giants back in October. After four long years of anticipation, it was time for sweet revenge.

The game, however, was a spitting image of the first matchup. It was a tough and physical game, and the Giants were somehow always able to frustrate the Patriots. When the Giants went up 9–0 in the first quarter, it was clear that New York just posed a bad matchup for the vaunted Patriots, and that if New England was going to win this rematch, they would have to be even better than they normally were.

The Patriots slowly took over the game, moving the ball with ease, and completed a Super Bowl record 96-yard drive to score a touchdown and take a 10–9 lead at halftime. At the start of the third quarter, they continued right where they left off, Brady marching the team straight downfield. He ended the drive by hitting Aaron Hernandez for a 12-yard touchdown, increasing the lead to 17–9. The Patriots, finally, were beginning to assert themselves and pull away.

Or were they?

The danger for the Patriots was simple: They appeared to have control of the game, but the score was still close. The Giants may not have been thought of as one of the first-class teams like the Packers, 49ers, or Patriots. But at one point or another, they'd beaten all of them, refusing to give in to intimidation. They had given up 17 straight points to New England, but it was still only a one-score game. All they had to do was keep it close, as they had done so often, and maybe the Patriots would crack. If they did, the Giants would be there to make them pay.

The Giants began to close the gap, brushing off the Patriots' touchdown drive and mounting one of their own that led to a field goal. 17–12. Then they got one step closer. On the following drive, the defense held up its end of the bargain as Justin Tuck sacked Brady on a three-and-out. Once more, Eli Manning led the Giants into field goal range, and Lawrence Tynes hit a kick through the uprights to make it 17–15. Heading into the fourth quarter, the game was up for grabs.

Just like in Super Bowl XLII, the conclusion of Super Bowl XLVI was unforgettable. It was the sort of ending that people will talk about for years to come. Really, for the Patriots, only one play on offense mattered. The moment came with 4:44 left in the game, the Patriots still up 17–15, facing a second-and-11 from the Giants' 44-yard line. Brady looked to his left and saw Wes Welker open on a deep slant.

Welker was the team's top receiver and one of the great Patriot weapons. He'd joined the team the year they went 16-0. He was known for his shiftiness and his great hands. He was also there when the Giants beat New England to steal the Patriots' chance at an undefeated season. Now he was there to make amends.

There was a hole in the defense and Brady, as he so often did, found it. The Giants had already used one time-out and the clock was ticking away. A Patriots first down would be a huge blow to the Giants' chance at making a comeback.

Brady threw behind Welker, who had to twist backward to reach the ball. He got two hands on it—but it slipped out of his grasp. The Patriots had no luck on third down, and instead of running out the clock, they were forced to punt.

The door was open for a Giants comeback, just like it'd been when the Patriots lost to the Giants back in October, and just like it'd been back in Super Bowl XLII.

Eli Manning took the ball from his 12-yard line.

On first down, Manning stepped back and uncorked a deep ball down the sideline. His receiver, Mario Manningham, was double-covered by safety Patrick Chung and cornerback Kyle Arrington. There was almost no room for the football to even fit. Yet Manningham reached over his shoulder, between two guys, and caught the ball at the very edge of the sidelines.

But everyone watching wondered the same thing: did he keep both feet inbounds?

After reviewing the play, the officials came back

out onto the field. The entire stadium looked on as the referee signaled a catch. Manningham had successfully tightroped along the sideline!

It was déjà vu for the Patriots, like the great David Tyree catch all over again, on another great throw by Manning. The Giants were now at midfield, 3:39 left on the clock. Manning hit Manningham again for 16 yards and then once more for another short gain. He was on fire now, throwing to Hakeem Nicks for 14.

Manning and the Giants could not be stopped. It was happening all over again to the Patriots. At the New England 18-yard line, Giants running back Ahmad Bradshaw ran for 7 yards. On the next play, Manning hit Nicks for 4 more yards. With the Giants so close to the end zone, the Patriots' defense, hoping to give its offense more time to come back out and score, decided to open up and allow Bradshaw to run up the middle for a touchdown with 1:04 left. Bradshaw realized what was happening and tried to fall at the 1-yard line so the clock would keep running, but his momentum propelled him into the end zone. The Giants had the lead again. It was 21–17 after a failed two-point conversion.

Despite New England's strategic decision, the desperate last drive for the Patriots failed. There simply wasn't enough time, and when Brady's final Hail Mary pass fell to the ground, the rematch was over. Neither revenge nor redemption could be found on this day. Twice the Patriots were favored to win the Super Bowl and twice the Giants overcame the odds. The Patriots were the most successful football team of the last ten years but had lost two Super Bowls in difficult fashion, left to wonder if Brady would ever win that fourth Super Bowl.

At the end of the day, for the second time in four years, it was Manning, not Brady, who was named the Most Valuable Player of the Super Bowl. It was Eli Manning who'd won two championships to big brother Peyton's one. Meanwhile, Tom Brady and the Patriots sat in the locker room, dejected, as Manning and his teammates hoisted the Lombardi Trophy once more. It was a different year, a different game, but the same result. On the final day of the season, the Giants stood tall yet again.

SUPER BOWL XLVI
TOP TEN LIST

Great rivalries are what sports are all about. Nothing gets fans more excited than a stand-off between bitter foes. The NFL has seen its fair share of epic duels throughout league history. Yet sometimes one great game just leaves us wanting more. Luckily, there have been some excellent rematches between rivals in the past. Here are the top ten greatest playoff rivalries in NFL history.

1. Dallas Cowboys vs. Pittsburgh Steelers: Faced off in the Big Game twice in four years in Super Bowls X and XIII. Pittsburgh won both games by 4 points.
2. Dallas Cowboys vs. San Francisco 49ers: Met in the NFC championship in 1992, 1993, and 1994. Dallas won the first two matchups before San Francisco beat them in the third.

3. Denver Broncos vs. Cleveland Browns: Back-to-back epic AFC Championship Games in 1986 and 1987. The Browns lost both in heartbreaking fashion to Elway and Co.

4. New England Patriots vs. New York Giants: Met in Super Bowl XLII and played a rematch in Super Bowl XLVI. New England was heavily favored in both games, but New York won twice with the help of a spectacular catch in the fourth quarter.

5. Oakland Raiders vs. Pittsburgh Steelers: Met in the playoffs *five straight years*, 1972–1976. Pittsburgh won three of the five matchups.

6. Tom Brady vs. Peyton Manning, 2001–present: The two best quarterbacks of their generation (seven league MVPs between them) have met four times in the playoffs, with a trip to the Super Bowl on the line three out of the four. Each has won twice.

7. San Francisco 49ers vs. New York Giants: These teams met four times in playoffs between 1981 and 1987. They split the series 2-2.

8. San Francisco 49ers vs. Green Bay Packers: Have you noticed that the 49ers appear on this list

a lot? They faced off against the Packers four straight years in the playoffs between 1995 and 1999. Green Bay won three of the four.

9. Dallas Cowboys vs. Minnesota Vikings: The Cowboys also appear on this list a lot! They met the Vikings four times in the playoffs between 1971 and 1977. Dallas won three out of four games.

10. Dallas Cowboys vs. Green Bay Packers: Dallas knocked Brett Favre and the Packers out of the playoffs three straight years from 1993 to 1995.

SUPER BOWL XLIX ONE TO REMEMBER, ONE TO FORGET

SEATTLE SEAHAWKS VS. NEW ENGLAND PATRIOTS

While the New England Patriots were blowing out the Indianapolis Colts in the AFC title game, the Seattle Seahawks were basking in the glory of a fantastic comeback against Green Bay in the NFC Championship Game. The defending champion Seattle Seahawks were going back to the Big Game. The Patriots were returning for the first time since suffering a second heartbreaking loss to the Giants four years prior.

New England versus Seattle was the dream matchup everyone in football wanted to see. The two best teams in the NFL were going to play for the Super Bowl.

There was a lot to be excited about in this fight between two giants. Pete Carroll, the Seattle head coach, had been the coach of the Patriots in the late 1990s before being fired and replaced by Bill Belichick. Belichick took over for Carroll and won three Super Bowls.

There was Russell Wilson, the young Seattle quarterback who had been making a name for himself as a big-game player and natural-born champion ever since entering the league three years earlier. The other members of the new generation of big-name quarterbacks, Andrew Luck of Indianapolis, Robert Griffin III of Washington, and Colin Kaepernick of San Francisco, were more highly touted, but unlike them, Wilson had proven that he could lead his team to a championship. During the regular season, Wilson and the Seahawks had outclassed their bitter divisional rival San Francisco, outplaying Kaepernick face-to-face in two matchups. In 2013 not only had Wilson led his team to a Super Bowl win, but he'd done so by beating the great Peyton Manning and the Broncos by a massive score of 43–8. Kaepernick, Luck, and Griffin may still evolve into championship quarterbacks . . . but Wilson? He already was one.

In the backfield, Wilson was supported by the great power running back, Marshawn Lynch. Lynch, nicknamed "Beast Mode" for his tenacious style of play, was known for breaking tackles and refusing to go down to the ground. Following a strong start to his career in Buffalo, Lynch struggled after injuring his shoulder in his second season. He eventually lost his starting job a year later. The next season, Lynch was traded to the Seahawks, and in Seattle, he found an opportunity to rejuvenate his career. He responded, getting voted into the Pro Bowl in four straight seasons and establishing himself as one of the top runners in the league. On the field, Lynch emerged as the workhorse of the team, and off the field, he became known as a character who routinely refused to speak to the media, but was still loved by fans for his excellent work ethic (and his love of Skittles).

Seattle was so good, the argument could be made that Wilson or Lynch weren't even the best players on the team. The Seahawks were loaded on defense. Every great defense needs a great nickname, in the tradition of the Doomsday Defense, the Purple People Eaters, and the Steel Curtain, and Seattle was no exception. Their defense, specifically their secondary, was known as the "Legion of Boom," and offensive players found out why when they got tackled with brutal force.

Safety Kam Chancellor hit like he could level a brick wall. His counterpart at safety, Earl Thomas, was a tackling machine. Linebacker Bobby Wagner wasn't just fast and powerful, he also had great hands and could intercept passes. Defensive ends Cliff Avril and Michael Bennett were hungry pass-rushers.

But the key to the defense was cornerback Richard Sherman. Sherman was a beast, so good that quarterbacks didn't even want to throw to his side of the field for fear he would intercept them, and he often did. Sherman was the personality of the defense: brash and full of smack talk, but so exceptional on the field that he backed it all up. Sherman followed the old line of "It isn't bragging if you can do it." That was evident by the fact that the Seahawks were playing in the Super Bowl for the second straight year.

In sports, it is so easy to throw around words like "dynasty," a term that should only be used for the rare teams whose greatness endures over many years. It is, however, overused, and after Seattle won one Super Bowl, with a chance to win another, people began to believe that maybe this Seahawks team was the next dynasty to be born.

Perhaps, but the team that held the better claim to that word was the Patriots, again in the Super Bowl, twelve years after their first championship victory, when Tom Brady and coach Bill Belichick upset the Rams. In those twelve years, they had established themselves as one of the greatest teams in the history of the NFL, reaching the Super Bowl six times. Yet more recently, they had suffered two heartbreaking Super Bowl losses to the Giants on incredible, clutch performances that no Patriots fan would soon forget. New England had the lead in those two Super Bowls in the final ninety seconds, only to lose both.

The Patriots played in their fourth straight AFC Championship Game in the 2014–2015 season, but they hadn't been back to the Super Bowl since their last loss to the Giants. And yet, here they were again.

Somehow, though, there was an added element of pressure this time around. Athletes can't play forever, not even the legendary Tom Brady, who was now thirty-seven years old. How many more chances would he have to win another title and join Terry Bradshaw and Joe Montana as the only players ever to win four Super Bowls? Earlier in the season, Brady and the Patriots hadn't played well. They'd had trouble beating bad teams, like Oakland, and were demolished by the mediocre Kansas City Chiefs in front of a national TV audience on *Monday Night Football*. The Patriots looked like maybe age had finally caught up to them.

Not so.

On February 1, 2015, seventy thousand people filled the University of Phoenix Stadium, the same site where the undefeated Patriots had lost to the Giants in Super Bowl XLII. The fans looked on with anticipation. How would the great Brady fare against the Legion of Boom? Could Wilson really win back-to-back Super Bowls by beating Manning and then Brady, the two defining quarterbacks of the era?

The Patriots moved the ball quickly, with short passes to Julian Edelman, Brady's quick slot receiver, and Rob Gronkowski, the hulking tight end with speed. The Patriots were poised to score first when the Legion of Boom made its first big play, an interception by cornerback Jeremy Lane on the goal line.

When Lane ran the ball back, however, he was tackled hard, broke his arm, and was out for the game.

The defenses then continued to control the game early. 0–0 at the end of the first quarter.

In the second, Brady attacked the Legion again, this time finding his tall receiver Brandon LaFell for an 11-yard score, and the Patriots led, 7–0. After the touchdown, the defenses settled in once more, each side holding the other to a three-and-out on their next possessions. Then it was Seattle's turn to strike. The Seahawks came right back and scored when Lynch rushed home from 2 yards out just before the two-minute warning.

The rigors of football take their toll, and it was clear that a season of bone-crushing hits were finally weakening the Seattle secondary. Sherman was essentially playing with one arm, the other crippled with torn elbow ligaments. His Pro Bowl teammate Earl Thomas had suffered a dislocated shoulder recently. Yet each soldiered on. And Brady struck again, slicing through the Seahawk defense and hitting Gronkowski, who barreled his way into the end zone for a 22-yard score.

By the time Seattle got the ball back, there were only thirty-one seconds left in the half. Instead of taking the conservative course and letting the clock wind down, the Seattle offense went to work, charging 80 yards down the field in a matter of seconds. Wilson struck right back, throwing an 11-yard touchdown to wide receiver Chris Matthews, a guy who hadn't made a single catch during the regular season. The game was tied at halftime. The Patriots' defense, just like in previous Super Bowls, hadn't been able to get a stop when it needed one. It was a demoralizing way to end the half.

After the second-half kickoff, Seattle took the ball down the field and moved to within striking distance, just inside the 10-yard line. New England's defense held strong, but Seattle hit a field goal to take the lead, 17–14.

On the next drive, Brady began to rush his delivery just slightly and was intercepted by Bobby Wagner deep in New England territory. Then Lynch took over, and the Patriots had no answer for Beast Mode. Wilson capped off the drive with a short touchdown pass to Doug Baldwin and suddenly it was 24–14.

On the sideline, Sherman could feel the Patriots cracking. "He's scared. His heart's gone. It's almost gone," he said of Brady.

Down by 10 points, it seemed as though the Patriots had no more answers for the Seahawks' attack. Seattle was too good. The Legion of Boom kept Brady from moving the football. In addition, there were surprise stars in the game, like Matthews, who had hardly played in the regular season and suddenly was the difference maker with 4 catches for 109 yards. Meanwhile, Patriots cornerback Logan Ryan, who was being attacked by Wilson, let up catch after catch and forced Belichick to make a change. The veteran coach inserted a little-used rookie, Malcolm Butler, into the game.

The third quarter ended. Seattle led, 24–14. The Seahawks were fifteen minutes away from repeating as champions, looking like a team that might really deserve to be called a dynasty.

Sherman said that Brady's heart was "almost gone," but whatever was left was beating strong. With twelve minutes left in the game, Brady decided not to throw the ball deep anymore, instead going with short passes underneath to quicker players who might have a better chance against the Seattle defense. He found his marks, hitting LaFell, Edelman, running back Shane Vereen, and Edelman again. Suddenly the Patriots were alive. At midfield, Earl Thomas grabbed Vereen's face mask for a 15-yard penalty and the Patriots kept driving. Brady found Edelman again and then another speedy receiver, Danny Amendola, for a 4-yard touchdown.

It was 24–21 with eight minutes left.

Seattle, needing to keep the ball and shave time off the clock, couldn't manage to control the game, and was forced to punt the ball back to the Patriots.

Brady took advantage, hitting Vereen three times and then Gronkowski for a big 20-yard gain, and the Patriots were at the Seattle 32 with 4:12 left.

Gronkowski beat Chancellor for 13 more yards and the ball was on the 19.

Vereen ran up the middle for 7 and LaFell caught and ran for 7 more.

The Patriots were on the Seahawks' 5-yard line with only 2:52 left. Belichick called time-out.

Seattle's defense needed to come through, and for

one play, at least, they did, stuffing a run at the 3. But then Brady called on Edelman again, who darted toward the middle of the field and faded to the sideline, where Brady hit him right in the hands for the go-ahead touchdown!

The Patriots, after being down 24–14 to start the final quarter, had scored two touchdowns and had the lead with two minutes to go!

But two minutes is a lot of time in a football game. Too much time for comfort. Could the New England defense get a stop and win the Super Bowl when it had failed to do so in the previous two matchups?

Could Wilson win a second Super Bowl and claim legendary status, following in the footsteps of Brady himself?

2:02 left. Seattle at its own 20. Lynch, the burly running back, lined up as a wide receiver and took off downfield. Wilson hit him and he went charging before linebacker Jamie Collins ran him down. Just like that, Seattle was at midfield with 1:55 left.

After a couple of incomplete pass attempts, Wilson found wide receiver Ricardo Lockette for 11 yards, bringing the ball to the Patriots' 38. As the Seattle fans grew more excited, Patriots fans had that familiar bad feeling in their stomachs. Could they really lose a third Super Bowl in the final minute?

Wilson dropped back with 1:14 left and threw down the right sideline. The young cornerback that Belichick had inserted in the game, Malcolm Butler, was there and made a great play to tip the ball away from the receiver Jermaine Kearse. Running at full speed, Butler and Kearse crumpled to the turf.

But Kearse kept his concentration. He kept watching the ball. Lying on his back, he tipped the ball to himself, juggled it, and then somehow caught it! Seattle had the ball on the 5-yard line with 1:06 left!

No one could believe it! It had happened again to the Patriots. A miraculous, impossible catch was about to doom them in the biggest game of the year. First David Tyree. Then Mario Manningham. And now Kearse.

New England fans couldn't stand to watch their hopes get crushed yet again.

Seattle went Beast Mode, and gave the ball to Lynch, who barreled his way toward the goal line, only to be stopped at the 1 by Dont'a Hightower.

The clock kept ticking down. Lynch expected the

ball. Everyone watching the game expected Lynch to get the ball. He was the toughest running back in the league. He had already rushed for 102 yards and scored a touchdown earlier in the game. He had nearly scored on the last play before Hightower stopped him.

Wilson looked up at the clock.

It read twenty-six seconds.

He took the snap, looked to his right . . . and threw!

No one was expecting a throw!

No one, that is, except Malcolm Butler, the kid who hadn't started the game. The kid who had done everything right, but had suffered a devastating moment of bad luck when Kearse made his magical catch. The kid who had been in college a year ago and now was playing in the Super Bowl.

He watched the play unfold. He watched Kearse dart inward, and then saw Brandon Browner, the Patriots cornerback, move up to block Kearse. The man Butler was guarding, Lockette, was going to get the ball, Butler saw, and immediately slanted toward the goal line.

Butler beat him to the spot, stepped in front of Lockette, and intercepted the ball on the goal line!

Just like that the game was over. The Patriots had won the Super Bowl by making the defensive play they could not make in the last two heartbreaking losses. Brady had his fourth Super Bowl championship, and in the twelve years from 2002 to 2014, the Patriots had been to six Super Bowls and won four of them. Brady joined Montana and Bradshaw as the only quarterbacks to win four Super Bowls, and solidified his place as perhaps the greatest quarterback to ever play the game. He had been brilliant in the fourth quarter, and the Patriots had become the first team to come back from a 10-point deficit in the fourth quarter to win a Super Bowl. The memory of losing those last two Super Bowls had finally, at least a little, been erased.

The Patriots were champions again.

Now it was Seattle who had suffered heartbreak of their own, failing to win another championship when they'd been just 1 yard shy of victory. The fans were crushed, and some very angry, because they believed had Lynch gotten the ball, the Seahawks would be champions today. It was not to be. On one side of the field, it was a day that would always be remembered. On the other, on the Seattle side, it was a day to forget. For the fans of football, however, the drama, win or lose, is exactly why people love the game. It's the reason we watch the action unfold week after week.

All culminating in the biggest, most important game of the year. The Super Bowl.

SUPER BOWL XLIX
TOP TEN LIST

Pete Carroll made the call. Russell Wilson threw the ball. The rest is history. With the championship on the line, one play decided the outcome and the Patriots sent the Seahawks home empty-handed. There's nothing like the biggest game of the year ending on the last play or in the final seconds. When it happens, it is unforgettable. Here are the top ten fantastic finishes in Super Bowl history.

1. New England Patriots vs. Seattle Seahawks, Super Bowl XLIX: Almost everyone watching on TV and in person expects Seahawks running back Marshawn Lynch to run the ball, including Lynch. But he never gets it. Instead, Patriots cornerback Malcolm Butler intercepts Seahawks quarterback Russell Wilson on the goal line. Patriots win.

2. San Francisco 49ers vs. Baltimore Ravens, Super

Bowl XLVII: With under two minutes to play, the Ravens' defense wins the Super Bowl, stopping the 49ers four times on the goal line.

3. Arizona Cardinals vs. Pittsburgh Steelers, Super Bowl XLIII: Steelers wide receiver Santonio Holmes makes maybe the greatest game-winning touchdown catch in Super Bowl history, just barely keeping both feet in bounds in the end zone.

4. Buffalo Bills vs. New York Giants, Super Bowl XXV: Bills kicker Scott Norwood misses a 47-yard field goal that would have won the game (talk about pressure!). Buffalo loses by a point.

5. San Francisco 49ers vs. Cincinnati Bengals, Super Bowl XXIII: 49ers quarterback Joe Montana leads an eleven-play, 92-yard drive. John Taylor hauls in the winning catch with half a minute left to play. The 49ers win the game by 4 points.

6. New England Patriots vs. New York Giants, Super Bowl XLII: Giants wide receiver David Tyree makes the greatest pressure catch in Super Bowl history, snagging the ball against his helmet as he falls to the ground. Four plays later, Eli Manning hits Plaxico Burress in the end zone for the game-winning score.

7. New England Patriots vs. New York Giants, Super Bowl XLVI: Giants wide receiver Mario Manningham makes the catch of his life, a 38-yard grab tiptoeing along the sideline at midfield. Eli Manning leads another scoring drive and finishes off the Patriots once again.

8. New England Patriots vs. St. Louis Rams, Super Bowl XXXVI: A minute and a half left. Tie game. Patriots' ball with no time-outs. Tom Brady drives all the way to the Rams' 30-yard line before spiking the ball to stop the clock. Seven seconds left. Kicker Adam Vinatieri hits a 48-yard field goal to win the game.

9. Indianapolis Colts vs. New Orleans Saints, Super Bowl XLIV: Down a touchdown, but driving into Saints territory, Peyton Manning has a second Super Bowl in his sights . . . until Tracy Porter intercepts him and runs the ball back for a 74-yard touchdown to seal the victory.

10. St. Louis Rams vs. Tennessee Titans, Super Bowl XXXIV: Rams linebacker Mike Jones stops Titans wide receiver Kevin Dyson on the 1-yard line as time runs out.

A TIMELINE OF FOOTBALL'S KEY MOMENTS (TOP 40 STYLE)

1. 1920: The American Professional Football Association (APFA) is founded in Canton, Ohio
2. 1922: The APFA is renamed the National Football League
3. 1929: The Green Bay Packers go 12-0-1 and win their first NFL title
4. 1943: It becomes mandatory for players to wear a helmet
5. 1946: Kenny Washington becomes the first African American player to sign an NFL contract, joining the Los Angeles Rams
6. 1946: An NFL rival, the All-American Football Conference (AAFC), is formed
7. 1950: The AAFC folds, but three surviving teams, the San Francisco 49ers, Cleveland Browns, and Baltimore Colts, join the NFL

8. 1957: Syracuse rookie running back Jim Brown makes his NFL debut with the Cleveland Browns and goes on to become one of the greatest players of all time

9. 1958: The Baltimore Colts defeat the New York Giants for the NFL title in a matchup that's been nicknamed "The Greatest Game Ever Played"

10. 1960: A new rival to the NFL, the American Football League, is formed

11. 1960: The Dallas Cowboys are founded and former New York Giants defensive coordinator Tom Landry is named the head coach

12. 1960: Former New York Giants offensive coordinator Vince Lombardi is named head coach of the Green Bay Packers

13. 1960: The Houston Oilers win the inaugural AFL championship

14. 1965: Former University of Alabama quarterback Joe Namath is selected first in the AFL draft and signs a three-year, $427,000 contract with the New York Jets, a professional football record at the time

15. 1966: The AFL and NFL agree to play an annual championship game beginning in 1967 called the

"Super Bowl," and plan a complete merger of the two leagues in 1970

16. 1967: The Green Bay Packers beat the Dallas Cowboys in the famed "Ice Bowl"

17. 1967: The Green Bay Packers beat Kansas City in the first-ever Super Bowl

18. 1969: The New York Jets become the first AFL team to win the Super Bowl, beating the Baltimore Colts 16–7

19. 1970: *Monday Night Football* debuts

20. 1972: The Miami Dolphins win the Super Bowl, completing the only undefeated season in NFL history, finishing with a record of 17-0

21. 1973: Buffalo Bills running back O. J. Simpson becomes the first running back to rush for 2,000 yards in a single season

22. 1974: The goalposts are moved from the goal line to the back of the end zone

23. 1978: The NFL expands from a fourteen-game regular season to a sixteen-game schedule

24. 1981: A substance known as "stickum," an adhesive that helped receivers (and defenders) catch the ball more easily, is banned

*Green Bay Packers head coach Vince Lombardi
(right) with Jim Taylor (left) and Bart Starr
(center). (1967)*

Joe Namath is greeted by fans after making good on his guarantee by defeating the Baltimore Colts in Super Bowl III. (1969)

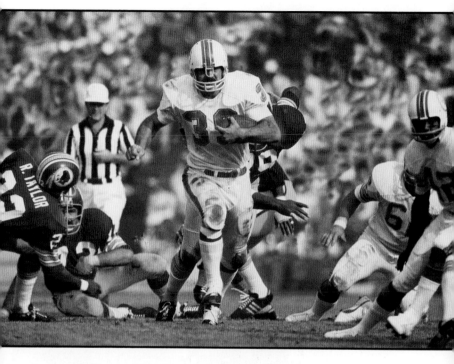

Larry Csonka rumbles through Washington's defense. (1973)

Sports Illustrated cover on January 26, 1976, celebrating Lynn Swann's incredible catch and the Pittsburgh Steelers' victory over the Dallas Cowboys.

Ken Stabler with head coach John Madden. (Yes, the same guy from the video game!) (1977)

"Mean" Joe Greene (left) and Jack Ham (right) of "The Steel Curtain" converge on the Dallas Cowboys' offense. (1979)

San Francisco 49ers' head coach Bill Walsh is raised on the shoulders of his players after winning Super Bowl XVI. (1982)

Chicago Bears defensive coordinator Buddy Ryan is held aloft by members of his defense, including (left to right) Otis Wilson, Richard Dent, and Dave Duerson. (1986)

Super Bowl XXII MVP Doug Williams celebrates following Washington's victory. (1988)

Jerry Rice en route to a familiar place for him—the end zone. (1990)

Joe Montana smiles before a game. (1990)

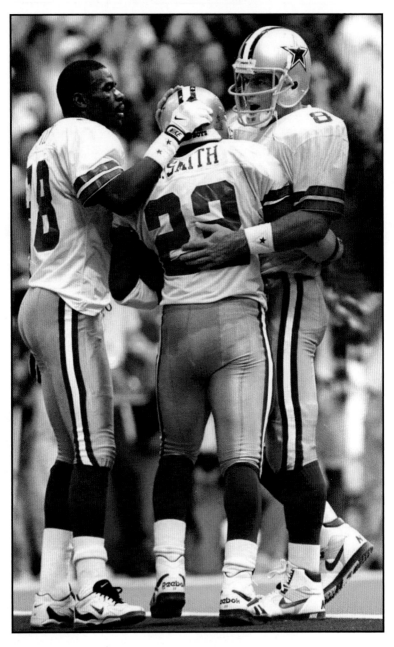

Michael Irvin (left) and Troy Aikman (right) congratulate teammate Emmitt Smith after he scores a touchdown. (1996)

Brett Favre and John Elway meet on the field before Super Bowl XXXII. (1998)

Kevin Dyson is tackled just inches away from the end zone as time expires, failing to score what would've been the game-tying touchdown. (2000)

Tom Brady loses the ball after being hit by Charles Woodson during the "Tuck Rule Game," but the referees rule the play an incomplete pass. (2002)

Tom Brady signals "first down" during Super Bowl XXXVIII. (2004)

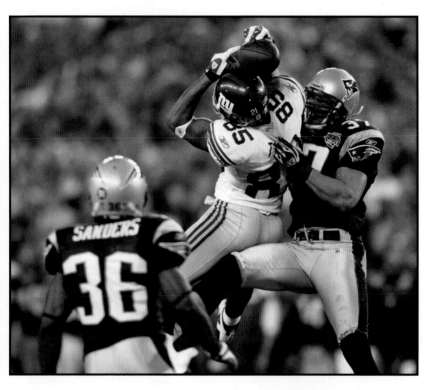

David Tyree makes his famous "Helmet Catch." (2008)

Eli Manning celebrates the New York Giants' victory in Super Bowl XLII. (2008)

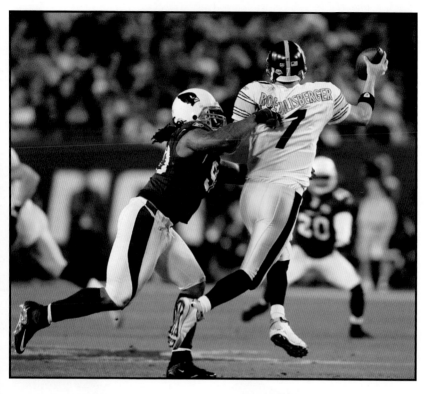

Ben Roethlisberger, under pressure, fights to stay on his feet. (2009)

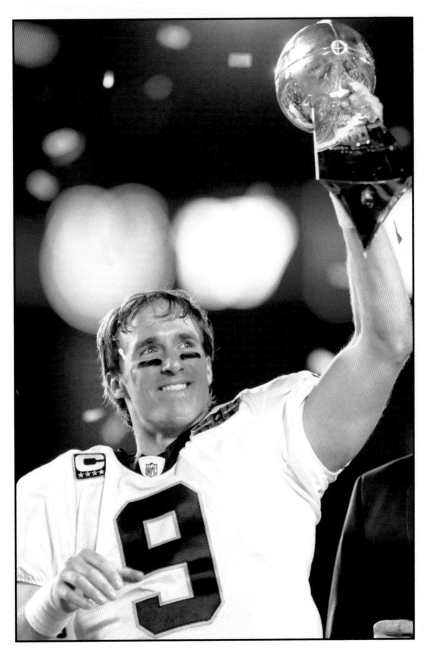

*Drew Brees celebrates after an emotional victory in
Super Bowl XLIV. (2010)*

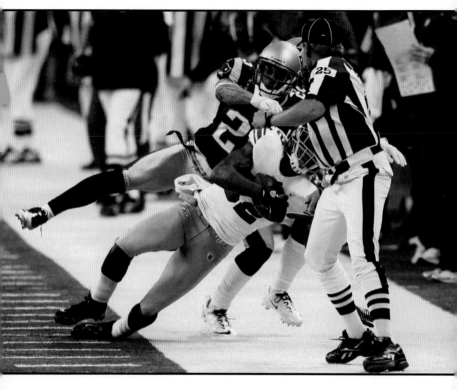

Mario Manningham tiptoes along the sidelines,
making an incredible catch. (2012)

*Malcolm Butler intercepts Russell Wilson on the goal line
(2015), sealing the Patriots' fourth Super Bowl victory.*

25. 1982: The Oakland Raiders move to Los Angeles, leaving the nation's second-most-populous city without a professional football team
26. 1982: Sacks become an official statistic
27. 1985: The Chicago Bears win their first championship since 1943
28. 1987: Bo Jackson becomes the first two-sport professional athlete of the modern era, playing both baseball and football
29. 1990: Joe Montana wins his fourth Super Bowl, tied for the most all-time by a quarterback
30. 1993: The Dallas Cowboys win the Super Bowl for the first time since 1978
31. 1994: The two-point conversion (as we know it today) is officially adopted by the NFL
32. 1995: The San Francisco 49ers win their fifth Super Bowl in thirteen years
33. 1997: The Green Bay Packers win their first Super Bowl since 1968
34. 2002: The "Tuck Rule Game" is played, in which the New England Patriots defeat the Oakland Raiders in the AFC championship on a controversial incomplete pass call that many people believe should have been ruled a fumble

35. 2002: The New England Patriots win their first-
    ever Super Bowl and the Brady-Belichick dynasty
    begins

36. 2006: The Pittsburgh Steelers win the Super Bowl
    for the first time since 1979, their fifth overall

37. 2007: The New England Patriots go 16-0 in the
    regular season, but lose the Super Bowl to the
    New York Giants

38. 2010: The NFL implements stricter rules to limit
    shots above the shoulders in an effort to reduce
    the risk of concussions

39. 2012: The NFL revises the sudden death overtime
    rules so that each team is guaranteed a possession
    unless a touchdown is scored on the opening
    drive

40. 2015: New England Patriots quarterback Tom
    Brady and coach Bill Belichick win their fourth
    Super Bowl title together

INDEX

A

All-American Football
Conference (AAFC), 3,
288
Adams, Bud, 171
Addai, Joseph, 251
Adderly, Herb, 5
"Air Coryell," 77, 88
Ali, Muhammad, 138
Alexander, Charles, 85, 242
Anderson, Ken, 242
Alzado, Lyle, 558
Amendola, Danny, 279
American Football
Conference (AFC), 22, 41,
42, 126, 149
Championship Games,
28, 50, 54, 97, 113,
152, 189, 218, 229–
230, 236, 267–268,
275
divisional playoffs, 50,
187, 229
title games, 32, 205, 222,
270
West division, 112
American Football League
(AFL), xiii, 4, 8, 13, 16–
17, 22, 49, 76, 172, 218,
228, 289
championship, 289
draft, 15
logo, 22
merge with NFL, 13–14,
25, 289–290
rivalry with NFL, 4,
9–10, 22
title game, 9, 17, 50
AFL-NFL World
Championship Game, 4
first, 6–7

second, 10
American Professional
Football Association
(APFA), 288
Aikman, Troy, 138–140, 142,
164, 220
Allen, George, 29–30
Anderson, Ken, 84–85
Arizona Cardinals, 150,
179–180, 254–255
centers, 237–238
offense, 237
quarterbacks, 234, 239
receiver, 237
running backs, 34
Super Bowl XLIII, 232–
240, 286
Arrington, Kyle, 264
Atkinson, George, 51
Atlanta Falcons, 6, 19, 48, 95,
161, 249
NFC championships, 229
NFC wild card game, 260
running backs, 35
Atwater, Steve, 157–158, 160
Avril, Cliff, 273

B

Baldwin, Doug, 277
Baltimore Colts, 3–5, 17, 179,
288
blitz, 18–19, 21
coaches, 11, 18–19, 26,
31–32
defense, 18, 21
NFL title game, 19, 289
quarterbacks, 4–5,
18–19, 26–27
Super Bowl III, 13–22,
198, 228, 290
Baltimore Ravens, 73, 180,
221, 236
AFC Championship
Games, 236
defense, 103, 286
linebackers, 103

Super Bowl XLVII, 243,
285–286
Banaszak, Pete, 52
Barton, Harris, 124
Bass, Mike, 31
Beebe, Don, 145–146,
Belichick, Bill, 11, 87, 97,
184–187, 191, 193–194,
203–205, 209, 211, 271,
274, 278–279, 281, 292
Bell, Todd, 123
Bennett, Cornelius, 144
Bennett, Michael, 273
Berry, Raymond, 18
Bethea, Larry, 83
Beyoncé, 9
Biekert, Greg, 188
Biletnikoff, Fred, 48, 52, 56
Biletnikoff Award, 52
Bledsoe, Drew, 183, 186,
190–191, 197
Bleier, Rocky, 41, 70
Blount, Mel, 41
Bly, Dré, 176
Boozer, Emerson, 16
Boston Braves, 180
Boston Patriots, 4, 97, 180, 182
Bradshaw, Ahmad, 265
Bradshaw, Terry, 41–42, 44,
65, 67, 72, 88, 163–164,
220, 258, 275, 283
Brady, Tom, 5, 87, 131,
193–197, 203–205, 207,
209–211, 236, 250, 257,
262–264, 266, 272, 292
Super Bowl XX, 97
Super Bowl XXVI, 228
Super Bowl XXXI, 255
Super Bowl XXXVI,
164–165, 185–191,
210, 287
Super Bowl XXXVIII, 199
Super Bowl XLII, 219–
221, 223–224, 230,
259, 261–264, 268,
275, 286–287

Brady, Tom (cont'd)
  Super Bowl XLVI,
    230–231, 257–266,
    268, 287
  Super Bowl XLIX, 274–
    276, 278–279, 283
Branch, Cliff, 52
Branch, Deion, 199, 210
Brees, Drew, 132, 164–165,
  247–248, 251–253
Brooks, Robert, 155, 160
Brown, Gilbert, 155, 159
Brown, Jerome, 123
Brown, Jim, 4, 34, 76, 289
Brown, Troy, 183, 195, 209,
  210
Brown, Willie, 51, 243
Browner, Brandon, 282
Bruce, Isaac "Ike," 167, 173–
  175, 177, 178, 190
Bryant, Paul "Bear," 15
Buckley, Terrell, 191
Buffalo Bills, 9, 27, 30, 47–49,
  181, 204, 221
  centers, 60
  coaches, 12, 88, 144
  defense, 144
  defensive ends, 103–104,
    144
  guards, 58
  head coach, 91
  kickers, 143, 146, 286
  linebackers, 144
  offense, 144
  quarterbacks, 88,
    144–145
  running backs, 30, 35,
    144–145, 290
  Super Bowl XXV, 286
  Super Bowl XXVII, 135–
    148, 149, 164, 256
  wide receivers, 144
Bunz, Dan, 84, 242
Burress, Plaxico, 227, 230, 286
Bush, Reggie, 247, 252
Butler, Malcolm, 242, 278,

  281–282, 285
Byrd, Isaac, 175

C

Campbell, Earl, 35
Candlestick Park, 141
Carolina Panthers, 154–155,
  235
  cornerback, 206
  defense, 209
  kickers, 207, 210
  quarterback, 202
  NFC title game, 203
  receivers, 202
  running backs, 202
  Super Bowl XXXVIII,
    199, 200–211
  tight ends, 210
  wide receivers, 202
Carroll, Pete, 271, 285
Carter, Anthony, 229
Carter, Cris, 47–48, 132
Casper, Dave, 52
"The Catch," 140
CBS, 9
Chancellor, Kam, 273, 279
Chicago Bears, 6, 14, 111, 135,
  182, 219, 230, 291
  coaches, 91
  defense ("46" defense),
    89–95, 99–101, 123
  defense captains, 93–94,
    103, 123
  defensive ends, 93, 102
  defensive tackles, 93, 102
  linebackers, 93, 102
  quarterbacks, 89
  Pro Bowl players, 93
  running backs, 35, 89
  safeties, 92–93
  Super Bowl XX, 89–101,
    127–128, 243
  wide receivers, 89
Chicago Cardinals, 233
Chmura, Mark, 155, 160
Christie, Steve, 145

Chung, Patrick, 264
Cincinnati Bengals, 47, 119,
  150
  defense, 85
  fullbacks, 85
  linebackers, 59
  offense, 167
  quarterbacks, 84
  Super Bowl XVI, 75–86,
    242, 255
  Super Bowl XXIII, 286
  tight ends, 85
  wide receivers coaches,
    76
Clark, Dallas, 205
Clark, Dwight, 77, 82–83,
  86, 140
Clark, Gary, 108, 114
Cleveland Browns, 3–4, 14,
  19, 28, 98, 111, 152, 180,
  268, 288
  AFC Championship
    Games, 112, 126,
    152, 267
  defensive ends, 58
  quarterbacks, 28, 111
  running backs, 4, 34,
    76, 289
Cleveland Rams, 179
coaches, 15, 106
  Baltimore Colts, 11,
    18–19, 26, 31–32
  Buffalo Bills, 12, 88, 144
  Chicago Bears, 91
  Dallas Cowboys, 7,
    11–12, 32, 65, 87,
    117–118, 137–138,
    289
  Denver Broncos, 88
  Green Bay Packers, 5, 11,
    88, 289
  Kansas City Chiefs, 12
  Miami Dolphins, 11–12,
    26, 95
  Minnesota Vikings, 88
  New England Patriots,

11–12, 87, 182–184,
203–204, 211, 255,
274, 292
New York Giants, 12,
182, 222, 229
New York Jets, 12,
31–32, 183
Oakland Raiders, 56, 182
Philadelphia Eagles, 101,
123
Pittsburgh Steelers, 12,
65–66, 88, 240
-quarterback
combinations, ten
best, 87–88
St. Louis Rams, 169, 186
San Diego Chargers, 8
San Francisco 49ers, 12,
77, 87, 117, 120, 129
Seattle Seahawks, 271
Tampa Bay Buccaneers,
256
ten greatest, 11–12
Washington, 12, 29, 108
Collins, Jamie, 280
Colston, Marques, 247–248, 252
Conwell, Ernie, 192
cornerbacks, 102–103, 118
Coryell, Don, 77, 88
Cotton Bowl, 78
Coughlin, Tom, 222, 229
Craig, Roger, 86, 118, 121,
127, 168
Cross, Randy, 86
Csonka, Larry, 26, 32–34, 76
Cunningham, Randall, 132

D

Dallas Cowboys, xi, 7–8, 30,
47–48, 56, 77, 79, 81–82,
90, 94, 109, 129, 149,
155, 160, 200–201, 203,
212–213, 222, 255–256,
267, 269, 289, 290, 291
"America's Team," 63–
64, 84, 87, 136, 148

center, 138
cheerleaders, 39
coaches, 7, 11–12, 32, 65,
87, 117–118, 137–138,
289
cornerbacks, 83
defense ("Doomsday
Defense"), 40, 42,
44, 66, 73, 81, 117,
136, 140, 273
defensive back, 42
defensive ends, 40, 83, 136
defensive tackles, 136
guards, 60
linebackers, 40, 83, 138,
241
NFC Championship
games, 140
NFC divisional playoffs,
231
NFC title games, 136
offense, 95, 243
Pro Bowl players, 136
quarterbacks, xi, 7,
39–42, 44, 65–66,
68–71, 83–84, 87,
136, 138, 141, 154,
163–164, 243
receivers, 41
running backs, xi, 34,
35, 65, 136, 139
Super Bowl V, 241
Super Bowl VI, 26, 28
Super Bowl X, 37–45, 63,
65, 163, 243, 267
Super Bowl XII, 65
Super Bowl XIII, 63–72,
163–164, 267
Super Bowl XXVII, 135–
148, 164, 256
tight ends, 67, 139
wide receivers, 7, 40,
138–139
Dallas Texans, 8, 180
quarterbacks, 8
Davis, Al, 51–52

Davis, Clarence, 52, 56
Davis, Kenneth, 145
Davis, Stephen, 202, 207
Davis, Terrell, 36, 132, 153,
156–161, 163–164
Dawson, Len, 8–9
DeBerg, Steve, 78
deep threats, 33, 52, 55, 202
defense, x, 167
Baltimore Colts, 18, 21
Baltimore Ravens, 103,
286
Buffalo Bills, 103–104, 144
Carolina Panthers, 209
Chicago Bears, 89–95,
99–103, 123
Cincinnati Bengals, 85
Cleveland Browns, 58
Dallas Cowboys
("Doomsday
Defense"), 40, 42,
44, 66, 73, 81, 83,
117, 136, 140, 273
Denver Broncos
("Orange Crush"),
53, 58, 74, 112–113,
132
Detroit Lions, 59
feats, ten greatest,
241–243
Green Bay Packers, 5,
102–103, 155, 158–160
Indianapolis Colts,
122–123
Los Angeles Raiders, 58
Miami Dolphins ("No-
Name Defense"), 26,
31, 74, 132
Minnesota Vikings
("Purple People
Eaters"), 39–40,
55–56, 73, 89, 132, 273
New England Patriots,
54, 183, 187, 190–
192, 209, 225–226,
265, 277–278

defense (cont'd)
New Orleans Saints, 91, 132, 252–253
New York Giants ("Big Blue Wrecking Crew"), 7, 73, 223, 258, 263, 289
New York Jets ("New York Sack Exchange"), 20, 74, 184
Oakland Raiders, 51
Philadelphia Eagles, 123
Pittsburgh Steelers ("Steel Curtain"), 12, 41–42, 44–45, 53, 64–65, 72–73, 89, 103, 240, 243, 273
players, top ten, 102–104
St. Louis Rams ("Fearsome Foursome"), 74, 169, 173, 192
San Diego Chargers, 132
San Francisco 49ers, 122, 127, 132
Seattle Seahawks ("Legion of Boom"), 73, 198, 273–274, 275–280
Tennessee Titans, 172, 174–176
Washington, 30–31, 108
Delhomme, Jake, 202, 206–210
Dent, Richard, 93, 102
Denver Broncos, 4, 66, 111–112, 143, 149, 198, 201, 213, 268, 271
AFC Championship Games, 112, 126, 152, 267
AFC divisional playoffs, 229
coaches, 88
defense ("Orange Crush"), 53, 74, 113, 132
defensive ends, 58, 112
linebackers, 59, 112
offense, 112, 131
Pro Bowl players, 112
quarterbacks, 88, 111, 113, 126, 132, 151–153, 161–162
receivers ("The Three Amigos"), 112
running backs, 35–36, 132, 153
safeties, 112, 157–158, 160
Super Bowl XXI, 152, 197–198
Super Bowl XXII, 105–116, 152, 197
Super Bowl XXIV, 119–130, 152, 164
Super Bowl XXXII, 151–162, 164
Super Bowl XLVIII, 198
tight ends, 132
Detroit, 84
Detroit Lions, 6, 47, 248
defensive tackles, 59
running backs, 34–35
Dickerson, Eric, 35
Didier, Clint, 115
discrimination in the game, 105–108, 115–116
Ditka, "Iron Mike," 91, 100–101
Dobler, Conrad, 58–59
Dorsett, Tony, xi, 35, 65–66, 68, 76, 136
"The Drive," 111–112, 149, 152
drugs, 182
Duerson, Dave, 93
Dungy, Tony, 117
Dutton, Big John, 136
dynasties, ten greatest, 212–213
Dyson, Kevin, 172, 176–177, 242, 287

E

Eason, Tony, 97, 100
Edelman, Julian, 275, 279
Eller, Carl, 55
Elliot, Lenvil, 82
Elway, John, 88, 111–114, 126, 132, 149–150, 151–152, 155–164, 229, 268

F

Fairbanks, Chuck, 182
Faulk, Kevin, 209, 220, 224
Faulk, Marshall, 131, 168–169, 185, 190–192
Favre, Brett, 88, 150, 154–156, 158–160, 164, 255–256, 269
fines, 60
Fitzgerald, Larry, 237–238
Foreman, Chuck, 55
Foster, DeShaun, 208
Fouts, Dan, 88
free agents, 110
Freeman, Antonio, 155–156
Fryar, Irving, 97

G

Gaffney, Jabar, 220
Garcon, Pierre, 253
Garrett, Mike, 8
George, Eddie, 172, 174–175
Georgia Dome (Atlanta), 171–172
Gibbs, Joe, 12, 108, 111
Gillman, Sid, 76
Glenn, Terry, 183–184
Gogan, Kevin "Big Nasty," 60
Gonzalez, Tony, 48, 117–118
Graham, Ben, 237
Graham, Daniel, 210
Grambling State University, 107
Grant, Bud, 88
"The Greatest Game Ever Played," 17, 289

Greco, Del, 175
Green, Darrell, 108
Green Bay Packers, 12, 14,
    30, 37, 38, 94, 150, 183,
    211–212, 260, 262, 268–
    269, 288, 290, 291
    coaches, 5, 11, 88, 289
    cornerbacks, 5
    defense, 5, 155, 159–160
    defensive back, 158
    defensive ends, 102–103,
        155
    defensive tackles, 155
    general managers, 154
    linebackers, 5
    NFC divisional round,
        190
    NFC Championship
        Games, 270
    NFC title game, 223
    offense, 155
    "Packer Sweep," 6
    Pro Bowl players, 155
    quarterbacks, 5–6, 88,
        256
    receivers, 5
    running backs, 5, 155
    safeties, 5, 157
    Super Bowl I, 3–10, 154,
        290
    Super Bowl II, 50, 154
    Super Bowl XXXI, 255
    Super Bowl XXXII,
        151–162, 164
    wide receivers, 155
Greene, "Mean" Joe, 23, 41,
    64, 103
Greenwood, L. C., 243
Gregg, Forrest, 5
Griese, Bob, 27, 33
Griffin, Don, 122, 142
Griffith, Howard, 159
Griffin, Robert III, 271–272
Grogan, Steve, 98, 100
Gronkowski, Rob, 47, 275–
    276, 279

Gruden, Jon, 256

H

Hakim, Az-Zahir, 167, 190–
    191, 193
Haley, Charles, 86, 144
halftime shows, 9
Hall, Dana, 142
Hall of Fame, 23, 30, 41, 46,
    48, 52–53, 55, 78, 93,
    102, 108, 129, 144, 149,
    163, 201
Ham, Jack, 42
Hamilton, Ray "Sugar Bear,"
    53, 187
Hampton, Dan, 102
Hannah, John, 98
Harper, Alvin, 139, 142
Harris, Bernardo, 158
Harris, Franco, 41, 65, 72, 76
Harris, Jackie, 174–175
Harrison, James, 59–60,
    234–235, 241
Harrison, Marvin, 205
Harrison, Rodney, 226
Hartwig, Justin, 237–238
Hayes, "Bullet" Bob, 7
Heisman Trophy, 8, 39, 65,
    247
"Helmet Catch," 230
Henderson, Devery, 247, 252
Henderson, Thomas
    "Hollywood," 40, 65
Hendricks, Ted "The Stork,"
    51
Hernandez, Aaron, 262
Hightower, Dont'a, 281
Hill, Tony, 66
Hilliard, Randy, 160
Holmes, Santonio, 237–239, 286
Holmgren, Mike, 88
Holt, Torry, 167, 177, 190
Hopkins, Wes, 123
Hornung, Paul, 5–6
Houston Oilers, 4, 66, 112,
    145–147, 171, 180

AFL championship, 289
    running backs, 35
    safeties, 58
Howard, Reggie, 208
Howley, Chuck, 241
Hurricane Katrina, 165, 245,
    249, 252

I

"Ice Bowl," 38–39
Incognito, Richie, 60
Indianapolis Colts, 17, 179,
    205, 205, 213, 219, 221
    AFC Championship
        Games, 218
    AFC title game, 205, 270
    defense, 122–123
    quarterbacks, 164–165,
        198, 241–242, 205,
        250, 250–253, 271,
        287
    receivers, 205
    running backs, 35, 205, 251
    Super Bowl XLIV,
        164–165, 198, 241,
        244–253, 287
    tight ends, 205
    wide receivers, 253
Irvin, Michael "The
    Playmaker," 47, 138–140,
    144, 220

J

Jackie's Place, 68
Jackson, Bo, 117, 291
Jackson, Mark, 112
Jacksonville Jaguars, 222
    AFC divisional playoffs,
        229
    coaches, 229
Jacobs, Brandon, 225
James, Craig, 97
James, Edgerrin, 205
The Joe Namath Show, 16
Johnson, Billy "White
    Shoes," 23, 117

Johnson, Calvin "Megatron," 47
Johnson, Jimmy, 12, 137–138, 140, 142, 147
Johnson, Vance, 112
Joiner, Charlie, 132
Jones, Brent, 121, 124, 142
Jones, Ed "Too Tall," 23, 40, 65, 83, 84, 136
Jones, Mike, 177, 242, 287
Jones, Rulon, 112
Jones, Tebucky, 192
Jurgensen, Sonny, 29

K

Kaepernick, Colin, 271–272
Kansas City Chiefs, 4, 37, 38, 48, 50, 130, 180, 275
    coaches, 12
    cornerbacks, 59
    quarterbacks, 8
    running back, 8
    Super Bowl I, 3–10, 290
    Super Bowl IV, 54
    wide receiver, 8–9
Kasay, John, 207, 210
Kearse, Jermaine, 281
Kearse, Jevon, 172
Kelly, Jim "Machine Gun," 88, 144–145, 147, 164
Kiick, Jim, 28
Kilmer, Billy, 29–31
Kraft, Robert, 182–184

L

LaFell, Brandon, 276, 279
Lambert, Jack, 41
Landry, Tom, 7, 11, 65, 69–70, 87, 118, 137, 289
Len, Jeremy, 276
Law, Ty, 183
league commissioners, 90
Levens, Dorsey, 155
Levy, Marv, 12, 88, 144
Lewis, D. D., 83
Lewis, Mo, 184

Lewis, Ray, 103
linebackers, 91, 103
linemen, 91
Lockette, Ricardo, 242, 280, 282
Lombardi, Vince, 5–8, 10–11, 38, 88, 155–156, 212, 289
Los Angeles Raiders, 98, 156, 179, 213, 291
    defensive ends, 58
    guards, 60
Los Angeles Rams, 14, 55, 66, 71, 90, 96, 125–127, 136, 179, 201, 288
    NFC division playoffs, 231
    offense, 131
    quarterback, 234
    running backs, 35
    Super Bowl XIV, 72
Los Angeles Memorial Coliseum, 4
Lott, Ronnie, 78–79, 86, 103, 122, 129
Luck, Andrew, 271–272
Lyght, Todd, 173
Lynch, Marshawn "Beast Mode," 272, 276, 278, 280, 281–283

M

Mackey, Joe, 18
Madden, John, 56, 149, 194
Madden NFL, 56
Manley, Dexter, 108
Mann, Charles, 108
Manning, Eli, 199, 221, 224–227, 230, 259, 263–266, 277, 286–287
Manning, Peyton, 5, 185, 205, 219, 221, 227, 259, 266, 268, 271, 275
    Super Bowl XLIV, 164–165, 198, 241–242, 250–253, 287
Manning, Ricky Jr., 206
Manningham, Mario, 230,

264–265, 281, 287
Marino, Dan, 95, 98, 132, 164, 230
Maroney, Laurence, 224
Marshall, Wilber, 94
Martin, Curtis, 183
Martz, Mike, 186
Mason, Derrick, 172, 176
matchups, top ten great, 163–165
Matthews, Chris, 197, 277–278
Matuszak, John "Tooz," 51
Maynard, Don, 16
McDowell, Bubba, 145
McGee, Max, 5
McGinest, Willie, 183, 192
McIntyre, Guy, 86
McMahon, Jim, 89, 90
McMichael, 93
McNair, Steve "Air," 172, 174–177
Meachem, Robert, 247, 252
Mecklenburg, Karl, 112
Meredith, "Dandy" Don, 7
Miami, 14, 42, 67
Miami Dolphins, xi, xiv, 34, 38, 38, 41, 48, 55, 95, 96, 98–99, 111, 147, 181, 213, 221, 228, 249, 290
    AFC Championship Games, 50, 230
    centers, 60
    coaches, 11–12, 26, 95
    defense ("No-Name Defense"), 26, 31, 74, 132
    guards, 60
    kickers, 31
    offense, 26
    quarterbacks, 27, 95
    running backs, 28, 34
    rushers, 26
    Super Bowl VI, 26, 28
    Super Bowl VII, 12, 25–33

Super Bowl VIII, 54
Super Bowl XVII, 108
Milloy, Lawyer, 183, 204
Minnesota Vikings, xi, 22,
    27, 32, 39–41, 44, 46, 48,
    94, 111, 125, 137–138,
    149, 171, 269
    coaches, 88
    defense ("Purple People
        Eaters"), 39–40,
        55–56, 73, 89, 132,
        273
    NFC championships,
        229
    NFC divisional playoffs,
        229
    Pro Bowl players, 55
    quarterbacks, 55, 88, 118
    receiver, 55
    running backs, 35, 55
    Super Bowl IV, 54
    Super Bowl VIII, 54
    Super Bowl IX, 40–41, 54
    Super Bowl XI, 49–57,
        163, 243
    wide receiver, 229
Mississippi Valley State, 121
Mobley, John, 160
Modell, Art, 180
Monday Night Football, 185,
    275, 290
Monk, Art, 108
Montana, "Joe Cool," xii, 23,
    78–83, 86–87, 119–120,
    123–130, 132, 140–142,
    150, 164, 196, 201, 220,
    255, 258, 275, 283, 286,
    291
Morgan, Stanley, 98
Morrall, Earl, 18, 21, 27–28
Morris, Mercury, 26, 33–34
Moss, Randy, 46–47, 131,
    132, 219–221, 225
Muhammad, Muhsin, 202,
    209
Murphy, Yo, 193

N

Namath, "Broadway Joe,"
    14–18, 20–23, 38, 228, 289
NFC, 42, 94
    Championship Games,
        40, 90, 108–109, 111,
        140, 171, 229, 254,
        270, 272
    divisional playoffs, 229, 231
    divisional rounds, 154,
        190
    East division, 136
    title games, 67, 71, 77,
        81, 96, 136, 203, 223,
        255, 260
    wild card game, 260
National Football League
    (NFL), xv, 3–4, 15, 32, 34,
    46, 49, 77, 98, 108, 147,
    182, 190, 233, 246–247, 288
    1967 Championship, 38
    contract negotiations,
        109–110
    Defensive Player of the
        Year award, 94, 104
    Defensive Rookie of the
        Year award, 172
    Dirtiest Player, 60
    Europe, 169
    merge with AFL, 13–14,
        25, 289–290
    rivalry with AFL, 4,
        9–10, 22
    Rookie of the Year
        award, 247
    rule changes, 166, 189,
        200–201, 292
    salary caps, 200–201
    seasons, 6, 66
    title games, 17, 19, 101
Nattiel, Ricky, 112–113
NBC, 9
New England Patriots, xi,
    xiv, 27, 46, 53, 92, 150,
    155, 180, 203, 213, 246,

248–249, 292
    AFC divisional games, 188
    AFC Championships,
        159, 218, 230, 274,
        291
    AFC title games, 205,
        222, 270
    coaches, 11–12, 87, 182–
        184, 203–204, 211,
        255, 274, 292
    cornerback, 192, 208,
        226, 278, 282
    defense, 190, 207, 209,
        225, 265, 277–278
    defensive backs, 183, 191
    defensive end, 54, 183,
        187, 192, 226
    "Greatest Show on Turf"
        offense, 166–180,
        185, 191, 193,
        228–229
    kickers, 189
    linebacker, 209
    linemen, 98
    NFC divisional round, 190
    offense, 131, 220
    quarterbacks, 5, 12, 87,
        97–98, 131, 190,
        192–197, 203–205,
        207, 209–211, 220,
        230, 236, 250, 257–
        258, 262–264, 266,
        272, 274, 283, 292
    receivers, 98, 190, 193,
        206, 220, 276, 279
    running backs, 97, 183,
        185, 190, 194, 209,
        221, 224
    safeties, 204, 226
    Super Bowl XX, 89–101,
        127–128, 243
    Super Bowl XXVI,
        228–229
    Super Bowl XXXI, 255
    Super Bowl XXXVI, 164,
        181–196, 210, 287

New England Patriots (cont'd)
Super Bowl XXXVIII, 199
Super Bowl XLII, 217–227, 230, 259, 261, 263–264, 268, 275, 286–287
Super Bowl XLVI, 230–231, 257–266, 268, 287
Super Bowl XLIX, 165, 197, 242, 270–285
tight ends, 47, 195, 276
wide receivers, 97, 183, 209, 219–221, 281
New Orleans, 99, 128, 245–246, 248–250, 252–253
Louisiana Superdome, 245, 247–248
New Orleans Saints
"The Ain'ts," 246
cornerbacks, 241–242, 253
defense, 132, 252–253
defense coordinator, 91
offense, 247
guards, 58
quarterbacks, 247
running backs, 35, 247
Super Bowl XLIV, 164–165, 241, 244–254, 287
tight ends, 247
New York Giants, 19, 81, 90, 109, 111–112, 126, 130, 143, 228, 236, 268, 274, 292
coaches, 12, 182, 222, 229
defense ("Big Blue Wrecking Crew"), 73, 223, 258, 263
defensive coordinators, 7, 289
defensive ends, 223, 223
linebackers, 118
linemen, 259

NFC Championship Game, 108
NFL title games, 17, 222, 260, 289
NFC wild card game, 260
offense, 259
offensive coordinators, 7, 289
quarterbacks, 221, 259, 264
receivers, 225, 263–264
running backs, 225, 265
safeties, 264
Super Bowl XXI, 152, 197–198
Super Bowl XXV, 286
Super Bowl XLII, 217–227, 230, 259, 261, 263–264, 268, 275, 286–287
Super Bowl XLVI, 199, 230–231, 257–266, 268, 287
tight ends, 224
wide receivers, 230, 287
New York Jets, 19–20, 27, 98, 199
AFL title game, 17–18, 50
clutch receivers, 16
coaches, 12, 31–32, 183
defense ("New York Sack Exchange"), 74
defense coordinator, 184
defensive captain, 20
linebacker, 184
quarterbacks, 14–16, 289
running backs, 16
Super Bowl III, 13–22, 31–32, 50, 198, 228, 290
Super Bowl XV, 198
nicknames
top ten defense, 73–74
top ten players', 23–24
Nicks, Hakeem, 199, 265
Nitschke, Ray, 5

Noll, Chuck, 12, 66, 72, 88
Norton, Ken Jr., 138, 140
Norwood, Scott, 143, 286
Notre Dame, 78
Novacek, Jay, 139

Oklahoma/Arizona Outlaws, 107–108
Oakland Raiders, xi, 10, 32, 38, 41, 46, 48, 179, 182, 198, 200, 202, 213, 268, 275, 291
AFC divisional games, 187
AFC Championship, 291
AFL title game, 17
coaches, 56, 182
cornerback, 51, 59, 243
defense, 51
guards, 60
linebackers, 51, 59, 188
linemen, 51
offense, 52–53, 167
quarterback, 52
receivers, 52
running backs, 35
running backs coaches, 76
safeties, 51, 58
Super Bowl II, 50
Super Bowl XI, 49–57, 163, 243
Super Bowl XV, 198
Super Bowl XVIII, 108, 164, 200–211
Super Bowl XXXVII, 256
offense, x, 80
Arizona Cardinals, 237
Buffalo Bills, 144
Cincinnati Bengals, 167
Dallas Cowboys, 95, 243
Denver Broncos, 112, 131
Green Bay Packers, 155
Los Angeles Rams, 131

Miami Dolphins, 26

New England Patriots, 131, 220

New Orleans Saints, 247

New York Giants, 259

Oakland Raiders, 52–53, 167

Pittsburgh Steelers, 167

St. Louis Rams, 131, 169, 178, 192

San Diego Chargers, 167

San Francisco 49ers, xii, 79, 81–82, 122, 131

Seattle Seahawks, 277

ten best, 131–132

Tennessee Titans, 172–173, 176

Washington ("The Hogs"), 108, 131

"West Coast," 86–87, 117, 129, 167

Ohio State, 172

"The Over-the-Hill Gang," 29–30

Owens, Terrell, 47

P

Page, Alan, 55

Parcells, Bill, 12, 182–184, 255

Parker, Willie, 198

pass catchers, ten greatest, 46–48

Patten, David, 190–191

Patterson, Elvis "Toast," 23

Payton, Walter "Sweetness," 24, 35, 89

Pearson, Drew, 40, 42, 44, 66, 70

Pearson, Preston, 66

Perry, Katy, 9

Perry, William "The Refrigerator," 93

Peterson, Adrian "All Day," 35

Phoenix Cardinals, 233

Phifer, Roman, 192

Philadelphia Eagles, 47, 71, 109, 123–124, 140, 180, 190, 201, 203–204, 211, 221, 235, 248

coaches, 101, 123

defense, 123

linebackers, 59

NFC title game, 203

safeties, 123

Super Bowl XV, 198

Phipps, Mike, 28

Pierre-Paul, Jason, 259

pioneers of the game, top ten, 117–118

Pitts, Elijah, 6

Pittsburgh, 28

Pittsburgh Steelers, xi, 50–51, 54–55, 126, 128, 147–149, 167, 170, 180, 189, 200–201, 213, 221, 255, 267–268, 292

AFC Championships, 159, 229–230, 236

blocking backs, 41

coach, 12, 65–66, 88, 240

cornerbacks, 41, 59

quarterbacks, 41, 88

defense ("Steel Curtain"), 12, 41–42, 44–45, 53, 65, 72–73, 89, 103, 240, 243, 273

defensive end, 64, 103, 243

fullbacks, 70

linebackers, 41–42, 59, 234, 241

linemen, 41

offense, 167

quarterbacks, 41, 65, 258

receivers, 41

running back, 65

safeties, 41

Super Bowl IX, 40–41, 54

Super Bowl X, 37–45, 63, 65, 163, 243, 267

Super Bowl XIII, 63–72, 163–164, 267

Super Bowl XIV, 72

Super Bowl XL, 198

Super Bowl XLIII, 232–240, 286

wide receivers, 65, 67, 286

Plank, Doug, 92

Plunkett, Jim, 198

Pontiac Silverdome, 84

Porter, Tracy, 241–243, 287

Pro Bowl players, 18

Proehl, Ricky, 167, 190, 193, 209–210

Q

quarterbacks, x, 18, 23, 46, 77, 80, 106, 167, 201, 211

Arizona Cardinals, 234, 239

Baltimore Colts, 4–5, 18–19, 26–27

Carolina Panthers, 202

Chicago Bears, 89

Cincinnati Bengals, 84

Cleveland Browns, 28, 111

-coaching combinations, ten best, 87–88

Dallas Cowboys, xi, 7, 39–42, 44, 65–66, 68–71, 83–84, 87, 136, 138, 141, 154, 163–164, 243

Dallas Texans, 8

Denver Broncos, 88, 111, 113, 126, 132, 151–153, 161–162

Green Bay Packers, 5–6, 88, 256

Indianapolis Colts, 164–165, 198, 241–242, 205, 250, 250–253, 271, 287

quarterbacks (cont'd)
 Kansas City Chiefs, 8
 Los Angeles Rams, 234
 Miami Dolphins, 27, 95
 Minnesota Vikings, 55,
  88, 118
 New England Patriots 5,
  12, 87, 97–98, 131,
  190, 192–197, 203–
  205, 207, 209–211,
  220, 230, 236, 250,
  257–258, 262–264,
  266, 272, 274, 283,
  292
 New Orleans Saints, 247
 New York Giants, 221,
  259, 264
 New York Jets, 14–16,
  289
 Oakland Raiders, 52
 Pittsburgh Steelers, 41,
  65, 258
 St. Louis Rams, 169
 San Diego Chargers, 88
 San Francisco 49ers, xii,
  78, 79, 87, 119–121,
  123, 128–130, 258,
  271, 286
 Seattle Seahawks, 271
 Tampa Bay Buccaneers, 107
 Tennessee Titans, 172,
  174–175
 Washington, 11, 29, 106,
  108–110, 116, 198, 271

R

Rathman, Tom, 124, 127
Raymond James Stadium
  (Tampa), 232
Redmond, J. R., 194
Reed, Andre, 48, 144, 146
Reich, Frank, 145–146
Reliant Stadium (Houston),
  201, 206
Relocated or changed names,
  ten teams that, 179–180

Replacement players, 110
Rice, Jerry, 46, 86, 121, 123,
  127, 129, 142, 219–220
Richards, "Golden," 40
rivalries, 217–227
 AFL-NFL, 4, 9–10, 22
 playoff, ten greatest,
  267–269
Robinson, Eugene, 159
Rodgers, Aaron, 272, 277
Roethlisberger, Ben "Big
  Ben," 198, 236–240
Romanowski, Bill, 59
Ross, Dan, 85
Rozelle, Pete, 90
rule-breakers, top ten, 58–59
running backs, x, 24, 80, 118
 Arizona Cardinals, 34
 Atlanta Falcons, 35
 Buffalo Bills, 30, 35,
  144–145, 290
 Carolina Panthers, 202
 Chicago Bears, 35, 89
 Cleveland Browns, 4, 34,
  76, 289
 Dallas Cowboys, xi, 34,
  35, 65, 136, 139
 Denver Broncos, 35–36,
  132, 153
 Detroit Lions, 34–35
 Green Bay Packers, 5,
  155
 Houston Oilers, 35
 Indianapolis Colts, 35,
  205, 251
 Kansas City Chiefs, 8
 Los Angeles Rams, 35
 Miami Dolphins, 28, 34
 Minnesota Vikings,
  35, 55
 New England Patriots,
  97, 183, 185, 190,
  194, 209, 221, 224
 New Orleans Saints,
  35, 247
 New York Giants, 225, 265

New York Jets, 16
 Oakland Raiders, 35
 Pittsburgh Steelers, 65
 St. Louis Rams, 35, 168
 San Diego Chargers, 132
 San Francisco 49ers,
  35–36, 86, 121, 142,
  242
 Seattle Seahawks, 72,
  272, 279, 280, 282,
  285
 ten best, 34–36
 Tennessee Titans, 172
 Washington, 114
Ryan, Buddy, 48, 91–92, 95,
  100–101, 123
Ryan, Logan, 278
Ryan, Rex, 91
Ryan, Rob, 91

S

safeties, 103
St. Louis Cardinals, 15, 19,
  180, 233
 guards, 58
 tight end, 67, 139
St. Louis Rams, 122, 170, 179,
  190, 203
 centers, 60
 coach, 169, 186
 cornerback, 176
 defense ("Fearsome
  Foursome"), 74, 169,
  173, 192
 defensive back, 173
 linebackers, 177, 242, 287
 NFC Championship
  Games, 171
 NFC title games, 255
 offense, 131, 169, 178, 192
 quarterback, 169
 receivers, 167–168
 running backs, 35, 168
 Super Bowl XIV, 72
 Super Bowl XXVI,
  228–229

Super Bowl XXXIV, 166–178, 242, 287

Super Bowl XXXVI, 164, 181–196, 210, 287

Saldi, Jay, 68

Sample Johnny, 20

Samuel, Asante, 226

San Diego Chargers, 167
AFC Championships, 229–230
AFC title game, 222
coaches, 8
defense, 132
guards, 60
offense, 167
quarterbacks, 88
running back, 132
tight ends, 132
wide receiver, 132

San Francisco 49ers, xii, 3, 14, 32, 46–47, 71, 87, 90, 93, 124–125, 141–143, 155, 160, 168, 170, 211, 212, 255, 262, 267–269, 288, 291
All-Pro players, 122
coaches, 12, 77, 87, 117, 120, 129
cornerback, 122, 143
defense, 122, 127, 132
guards, 60
linebackers, 59, 122, 242
linemen, 86, 124
NFC Championship game, 140
NFC divisional playoffs, 229
NFC title games, 260
offense, xiv, 79, 81–82, 122, 131
Pro Bowl players, 86
quarterbacks, xii, 78, 79, 87, 119–121, 123, 128–130, 258, 271, 286
receivers, 86, 167

running backs, 35–36, 86, 121, 142, 242

safeties, 103, 122, 143

Super Bowl IV, 152

Super Bowl XVI, 75–86, 242

Super Bowl XXIII, 286

Super Bowl XXIV, 119–130, 164

Super Bowl XLVII, 243, 257–266, 285–286

tight ends, 121, 142

wide-out, 78

wide receivers, 78, 121, 219, 260

San Jose State University, 76

Sanders, Barry, 34–35

Sanders, Deion "Prime Time," 24, 102, 118

Sanders, Ricky, 108, 114

Sauer, George, 16, 21

Schaefer Stadium, 53

Schroeder, Jay, 109–111

Seattle Seahawks, 46, 150
coaches, 271
cornerbacks, 273–274, 276, 281, 285
defense ("Legion of Boom"), 73, 198, 273–274, 275–280
defensive ends, 273
linebackers, 273, 281
NFC Championship Games, 270
offense, 277
Pro Bowl players, 272
quarterbacks, 271
running backs, 72, 272, 279, 280, 282, 285
safeties, 273, 279
Super Bowl XL, 198
Super Bowl XLIX, 165, 197, 198, 242, 270–285
wide receivers, 277, 280

Seifert, George, 120, 129

Shanahan, Mike, 88

Sharpe, Shannon, 132

Shell, Art, 52

Sherman, Richard, 273, 276, 278

Shockey, Jeremy, 247, 252

Shotgun formation, 118

Shula, Don, 11, 18–19, 21–22, 26, 31–32, 95–96

Simms, Phil, 197–198

Simpson, O. J. "The Juice," 30, 35–36, 76, 181, 290

Singletary, Mike, 93–94, 102–103

Smith, Antowain, 208

Smith, Bruce, 103–104, 144

Smith, Bubba, 18

Smith, Dennis, 112, 115

Smith, Emmitt, 34, 138–142, 144

Smith, Jackie, 67–70, 72

Smith, Malcolm, 198

Smith, Steve (Carolina Panthers), 202–203, 207, 227

Smith, Steve (New York Giants), 226

Smith, Timmy, 114, 197

Snell, Matt, 16, 21, 198

Solomon, Freddie, 78, 82–83

"Sprint Right Option," 82–83

"Squish the Fish," 99

Stabler, Ken "The Snake," 52–54, 56, 163

Stallworth, Donté, 220

Stallworth, John, 41, 65, 67

Stanford University, 77

Starr, Bart, 5–8, 38, 88

Staubach, Roger "Captain Comeback," xi, 66, 68–71, 87, 136, 141, 164
Super Bowl X, 39–42, 44–45, 65, 163, 243

Stepnoski, Mark, 138

Stickum, 290

Strahan, Michael, 223, 225, 227, 258
Suh, Ndamukong, 59
Super Bowl
I, 3–11, 154
II, 10–11, 154
III, 13–22, 198
IV, 22, 54
V, 241
VI, 11, 26
VII, 12, 25–33
VIII, 54
IX, 40–41, 54
X, 37–45, 46, 63, 65, 163, 267
XI, 48–66, 163, 243
XII, 11
XIII, 63–74, 163–164, 267
XIV, 72
XV, 198
XVI, 75–88, 242
XVIII, 164
XX, 89–104, 127–128, 243
XXI, 152
XXII, 105–116, 117–118, 152
XXIII, 286
XXIV, 119–132, 152, 164
XXV, 286
XXVI, 228–229
XXVII, 135–150, 164, 256
XXXI, 255
XXXII, 151–165
XXXIV, 166–180, 200–211, 242, 287
XXXVI, 164, 181–199, 210, 287
XXXVII, 256
XXXVIII, 199–213
XL, 198, 236
XLII, 217–231, 259, 261, 263–264, 268, 273, 286–287
XLIV, 164–165, 241, 244–266, 287
XLIII, 199, 232–243, 286
XLVI, 230–231, 257–269, 287
XLVII, 243, 285–286
XLIX, 165, 242, 270–284
50, xiii
finishes, top ten, 285–187
Most Valuable Player (MVP) Award, 18, 44, 56, 84, 120, 132, 161, 196, 198–199, 241, 266, 268
overtime, 159, 189
rings, 141, 250
Sunday, 37, 45
"The Super Bowl Shuffle," 90
surprise performances, ten greatest, 197–199
suspensions, 60
Swann, Lynn, 41–44, 46, 56, 65, 67, 220

T

Talbert, Diron, 30
Talley, Darryl, 144
Tampa Bay Buccaneers, 92, 201–202, 222, 255–256
coaches, 256
NFC Championship Games, 171
NFC title game, 255
quarterbacks, 107
Super Bowl XXXVII, 256
Tarkenton, Fran, 38, 55, 88, 118, 163
Tatum, Jack "The Assassin," 24, 51, 56, 58
Taylor, Charlie, 30
Taylor, Jim, 5–6
Taylor, John, 120–121, 124–125, 127, 286
Taylor, Lawrence, 103, 118
Taylor, Otis, 8
Television commercials, 9, 64
Tennessee Oilers, 180
Tennessee Titans, 150, 180,
190
defense, 172, 174–176
defensive end, 172
kickers, 175
offense, 172–173, 176
Pro Bowler players, 172
quarterbacks, 172, 174–175
receivers, 172, 242
running backs, 172
Super Bowl XXXIV, 166–178, 242, 287
tight ends, 172, 175
wide receiver, 175, 287
Thomas, Adalius, 226
Thomas, David, 252
Thomas, Earl, 273, 276, 279
Thomas, Pierre, 247, 251–252
Thomas, Thurman, 144
Tomlin, Mike, 240
Toomer, Amani, 225
Tuck, Justin, 223, 259, 263
"Tuck Rule Game," 188, 291
Tynes, Lawrence, 261, 263
Tyree, David, 224, 225–226, 230, 265, 281

U

Umenyiora, Osi, 223, 259
uniforms, xi, 42
Unitas, Johnny "U," 5, 18, 21–22, 26–27
United States Football League, 107–108, 136–137
University of Alabama, 15, 289
University of Arizona, 9
UCLA, 138
University of Colorado, 182
University of Florida, 139
University of Miami, 137–138
University of Michigan, 9
University of Phoenix Stadium, 275
University of Pittsburgh, 65
University of Southern California, 8, 79–80, 247

upsets, ten most memorable, 228–231
Upshaw, Gene, 52

V

van Eeghen, Mark, 52
Vereen, Shane, 279
Vermeil, Dick, 169–170
Vinatieri, Adam, 189, 195, 210, 287
Vince Lombardi Trophy, 10–11, 65, 156, 219, 266
Vrabel, Mike, 209

W

Wagner, Bobby, 273, 277
Walker, Herschel, 136–139
Walls, Everson, 83
Walsh, Bill, 12, 76–80, 82, 84, 86, 87, 117, 120, 129, 167, 255
Walter, Michael, 122
Ward, Hines, 198
Warner, Kurt, 131, 164–165, 169–171, 173–175, 177, 185–186, 190–193, 228, 234, 237–238, 240–241
Washington, xii–xiii, 38, 48, 55, 71, 90, 101, 126, 129, 143, 156, 180, 249
   coaches, 12, 29, 108
   cornerbacks, 108

defensive backs, 31
defensive ends, 108
defensive tackles, 30
NFC Championship Game, 108–109
offense ("The Hogs"), 108, 131
quarterbacks, 11, 29, 106, 108–110, 116, 198, 271
running backs, 114
Super Bowl XXII, 152
Super Bowl VII, 25–33
Super Bowl XVII, 108
Super Bowl XVIII, 108, 164
Super Bowl XXII, 105–116, 197
tight ends, 115
wide receivers, 30, 108
Washington, Kenny, 288
Washington, Mark, 42
Washington, Nate, 238
Washington State, 183
Watt, J. J., 104
Watters, Ricky, 142
Wayne, Reggie, 205, 253
Welker, Wes, 220–221, 224, 263–264
"West Coast Offense," 86–87, 117, 129, 167
White, Danny, 71, 84

White Randy, 65, 136
White, Reggie "Minister of Defense," 23, 102–103, 123, 155, 159
White, Sammy, 55–56
Wiggins, Jermaine, 195
Williams, Doug, 106–108, 110–111, 113–117, 198
Williams, Kyle, 260–261
Williams, Tyrone, 158
Williamson, Fred "The Hammer," 59
Wilson, Mike, 125
Wilson, Otis, 93–94
Wilson, Russell, 165, 242, 272, 273, 275–277, 280–281, 285
Winslow, Kellen, 132
Wisniewski, Steve, 60
Wolf, Ron, 154
Wood, Willie, 5
Woodson, Charles, 188
Woodson, Rod, 103
World's Strongest Man competition, 51
Wycheck, Frank, 172, 176

Y

Yepremian, Garo, 32
Young, Steve, 129, 141–142, 148, 201

ALSO BY HOWARD BRYANT

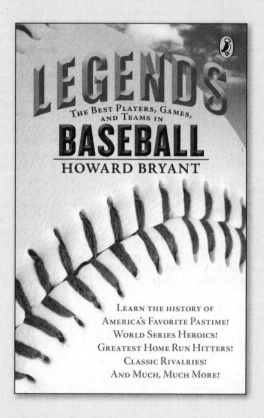